# Fat-free
## *gourmet recipes*

WHITE STAR PUBLISHERS

TEXTS
MAURIZIO CUSANI

PHOTOGRAPHS AND RECIPES
CINZIA TRENCHI

EDITORIAL DIRECTOR
VALERIA MANFERTO DE FABIANIS

EDITORIAL COORDINATION
LAURA ACCOMAZZO
FEDERICA ROMAGNOLI

GRAPHIC DESIGN
PAOLA PIACCO

# PREFACE
## by Maurizio Cusani

Throughout history, longevity and good health have always been considered among the most important objectives. As far back as the 7th century, the great Chinese doctor Sun Simiao (581-682 a.d.) advocated the consumption of nothing more than a vegetable soup at midday and even less in the evening, so as to leave the dining table not quite satiated. Moreover, he suggested that one should eat less and less as one's age increases. Modern studies have proved that the habit of eating very little, especially in the evening, and in a balanced manner, reducing the amount of food consumed over the years, is, in fact, one of the most effective ways to live longer and in good health. But this is not enough, of course.

Everything that enters into us, "becomes" us. Therefore, it is extremely important to eat healthy and natural foods, as we did in ancient times. A friend of mine, the son of a fisherman, once told me that when he was a child his family was very poor, and they could hardly ever afford to eat meat. And yet they never got ill: the diet that he and his family followed was in fact ideal. His father bartered the fish he caught with farmers along the coast, in exchange for olive oil, vegetables and fruit. Today, in spite of being financially much better off than he was back then, he is no longer able to eat as well, as he is unable to find fresh fish, oil, fruit and vegetables of the same quality. Nowadays, in developed countries, eating healthy genuine food has become an increasingly difficult objective: the use of pesticides, preservatives, hormones, antibiotics and colourings in agriculture, animal husbandry and the preparation of food, and in particular the greater consumption of packaged foods and fats, often excessively flavored and over-sweetened, have created the ideal breeding ground for tumours and diseases such as diabetes, high cholesterol and obesity.

How can we protect ourselves from these risks? First of all, it is important to choose seasonal fruit and vegetables, if possible "organic" produce, which has not been subjected to chemical treatments (various surveys suggest that the substances used penetrate deep into the flesh of the produce, and impede the consumption of the skin, which is rich in nutrients). In the natural world, apples are not perfectly round and red, but a little lumpy and irregular; and yet, they are tastier and more full of flavor, even though less visually attractive. It is a good idea to eat "live" foods, such as fruits and vegetables, straight after they have been picked, or as soon as possible after harvesting. Among other things, those who consume fresh fruit and vegetables are less likely to suffer from eye pathologies such as cataracts and macular degeneration. Yoghurt too is a food rich in highly useful and non-hazardous live bacilli. And there is even a type of wine that is defined "*vino vivo*": free of additives and preservatives, today it has become very rare, and is only produced in very small quantities for family consumption or by part-time growers.

But let's see what we should be doing regarding our consumption of meat. Man was originally born an omnivore and a gatherer. It is known that the teeth of our ancestors of 30-40.000 years ago were healthy because they ate foods that were raw, hard and fresh: berries, nuts, fruit, plants, and a small quantity of meat from wild animals. Of our 32 teeth, we have only 4 canines capable of piercing meat, and this information should clearly indicate that this food should make up only a small percentage of our diet – an amount that it is not advisable to exceed. Still on the subject of teeth, human beings once had 12 molars suited to slowly grinding foods that could only be absorbed by prolonged chewing, necessary to facilitate their digestion. Today, easy to absorb foods, lacking in fibre, are swallowed down in haste because there is no time for a proper lunch break or for a quick breakfast, if that meal still even exists. And no one teaches children that–, as well as the fact that a poor diet can lead to constipation, gastritis and irritable colon,– "the first stage of digestion takes place in the mouth". To digest effectively, significant chewing is required, and it is therefore necessary to use all teeth equivalently: this can occur only with the consumption of hard foods that are chewed for a long time. The modern diet, on the contrary, consists mainly of soft foods which, to some extent, "go down" easily. This means less chewing, less jaw exercise and less need for functioning molars, especially the third (and last) molars – the wisdom teeth – which develop latest. This is why wisdom teeth are becoming obsolete, and when they do grow, it is a decidedly painful matter!

Moreover, young people are no longer aware of nature's schedules and seasons. Very few children who live in the city have seen free range hens and cows. At primary school, many of them don't even know where their eggs or omelettes come from.

With regards to fish, most of those that we eat are bred in fish farms. Often their meat, rich in unsaturated fatty acids (which help to prolong life), is polluted with toxic substances such as mercury and other heavy metals. Today, fortunately, scientific knowledge can come to our aid in this regard: we are able, for example, to assess the doses of certain enzymes present in the flesh of farmed fish, in order to understand whether they have been treated in accordance with regulations, or if they have suffered. In fact, not all meats share the same qualities. It is unfortunate that these techniques are only accessible to a limited number of researchers; and although we are obliged to take a leap of faith, we should, however, develop our own awareness and knowledge.

Eating healthily and naturally has become increasingly difficult, and it is therefore necessary to find trusted suppliers, and to strive to be well informed about the culture of nutrition. Unfortunately, in recent years Western countries have witnessed a considerable shrinking of traditional farming and peasant culture. Today, many wines, including those that have earned the Registered Designation of Origin (DOC) status, seem to have the same taste and aroma; and can sometimes contain massive amounts of diluted preservatives and anti-mould agents. Once upon a time the wine we drank was "genuine", deriving directly from pressed grapes. When I was a child, in the evening my grandfather would dunk my piece of bread in his wine in order to give me strength... today it is difficult even to find good fresh bread, being often sold precooked or frozen. Besides, we all know that a glass of red wine a day improves the blood circulation and may reduce the risk of thrombosis and heart attacks in healthy subjects (but here too moderation is required).

To recap, we don't drink genuine wine, and we buy industrially produced, liver-damaging spirits, the fats of which end up in our adipose tissue. Or we consume sugary drinks rich in caffeine that can become addictive. There are numerous foods and drinks on sale that are high in protein or contain added vitamins. It is a know fact that those who eat fruit and vegetables already assimilate sufficient vitamins, and that even these, if consumed in excess, can be harmful to one's health. It is also well known that the most thirst-quenching drink available is water, and that we should drink at least 2 litres of it a day, preferably still (drinking plenty of still water does not make us put on weight or feel bloated). During the summer, it is wise to consume even more liquids, possibly freshly squeezed fruit juices, to compensate for the salts lost through perspiration. Drinking water helps to reduce the sensation of hunger, facilitates movement through the intestines, and promotes renal functioning, thus reducing the risk of kidney stones and gallstones. Carbonated water is something entirely different: it inflates the stomach and promotes bloating. And then, we must ask ourselves where this water comes from: are we sure that our tap does not give us a better product than the one sold to us in plastic bottles that perhaps come from 500 miles away?

One last statistic: we must also consider that we are in continuous evolution, and that we are not all equal, we do not all live in the same climates, and we do not all do the same type of work. Each country has its own habits and cultures. Societies are different, and their eating habits tend to adapt to these differences, usually wisely. In addition, every age has its own diet. Meat is much more suitable to growing bodies, such as adolescents rather than the elderly. Moreover, preventing the accumulation of fat in the elderly, among other things, helps to prevent blindness. Similarly, higher fat diets are better sustained by teenagers who undertake sporting activities than sedentary adults.

Having said this, however, our eating habits should not depress us. Numerous studies have demonstrated that optimism helps us to live longer and in good health. The propensity to be happy and in a good mood reduces the risk of cardiovascular disease and cancer, illnesses that constitute the majority of the causes of death in advanced age in western countries. Some statistics say that optimists live an average of 12 years more than pessimists, and with a better quality of life, especially in old age. Positive thinking, therefore, reduces stress and enhances the body's natural defences, while all negative emotions, and in particular an innate tendency to "see the glass half empty", is detrimental to our physical condition. It is true that abstinence, intermittent fasting and a reduced quantity of food are important factors for our longevity, but it is equally true that our food choices should be accepted with joy and without excessive fundamentalism, which could prove detrimental to our mood. In short, some exceptions to the rule, as long as they do not become the norm, are both welcome and healthy, as suggested by Woody Allen's famous aphorism: "I quit smoking, drinking and having sex; I will live one week longer, and that week it will rain every day".

The purpose of this book is to find the right balance between health and happiness, providing all the relevant information to help us to choose a life and eating culture that is most suitable to our specific needs, and that can make us happy without harming us physically. A conscious approach to food can improve our health and increase our vital energy. To this end, we have put together some useful tips for the preparation of simple, tasty and healthy dishes, in order to transform our eating habits into a therapeutic factor that will benefit our well-being and physiques.

# CONTENTS

# INTRODUCTION

ENERGY AND CALORIES

To live, human beings consume energy that comes essentially from food. Each food is made up of nutritional elements– i.e. sugars (carbohydrates), fats (lipids), proteins, vitamins and minerals,– that can be measured in calories. All of these substances contribute to supporting life by replacing damaged tissues, defending the body from external aggression, regulating the metabolism and, during childhood, facilitating growth.

The energy balance of the human body is determined by the ratio of calories introduced into the body and the calories burned, which should be equal: otherwise, an imbalance will lead to weight gain (up to obesity) if there is an excess of calories introduced, or weight-loss if there is an excess of calories burned.

The body of an average 30-year old adult male, measuring 5 foot 9 (175 cm) and weighing 11 stone (70 kg), is made up of just under 60% water, 20% protein, 16% fat, 4% minerals and 1% sugar, and contains traces of vitamins. In females, the percentage of fats is double and the lipids tend to increase with age. Water, which makes up 80% of the weight of a newborn baby, decreases, however, as the years pass.

Proteins are used primarily to create the structure of the body and to preside over the numerous and complex processes of metabolism, for example through enzymes (which are actually proteins). Sugars are transformed into glucose and glycogen, which act as fuels for the tissue. Fats, finally, represent the energy reserves to be used only in times of need.

Sugars, therefore, ensure a rapid and immediate source of energy, while fats should be used only in emergency situations, as they release energy with great difficulty. But if excess sugars are not consumed quickly, they transform into fat tissue. The energy of a food is measured in calories; the greater the energy of a certain food, the higher the number of calories. This energy is required by the muscles to perform physical activities. A piece of cake has a very high energy content, whereas that of carrots and celery is much lower: a small slice of cake, therefore, has a much greater caloric impact than a huge plate of raw celery and carrots.

As a result, the more high energy foods you eat, the more weight you put on, because the body does not do enough exercise to burn off the excess energy introduced. This energy surplus is stored in the adipose tissue, i.e. in body fat, which is very difficult to shift, because when one simply stops eating, the body first uses its sugar and protein reserves.

That is why losing weight in terms of water and lean body mass is very fast and easy, while losing weight in terms of fat mass is much more difficult. This goal can only be achieved slowly and with adequate physical exercise. Carbohydrates (or sugars, or glucids) and proteins provide 4 calories per gram, while alcoholic drinks 7 and fat 9. Fibre, vitamins, minerals and water have no calories at all. It is clear, therefore, that to lose weight you will need to do physical exercise and at the same timegive priority to foods with the lowest number of calories, i.e. fibres, vitamins, minerals, water, carbohydrates and proteins.

Sometimes, when people decide to lose weight, they reduce their intake of fat, but often, and almost subconsciously, they increase their intake of sugars, to create a substitute form of gratification. The effect is disastrous, because while fats are digested slowly, sugars are digested very quickly, and are less capable of satiating our appetite. As a result, dieters actually risk increasing their intake of calories, which are then transformed into fats: paradoxically, in this case the reduction of fat... can make you get fatter!

Fortunately, every psycho-physical activity burns calories. A person weighing 11 stone (70 kg) will consume 35 calories watching television for 30 minutes, 40 while reading, 80 while walking, 90 cooking, 130 walking at a brisk pace, 140 fishing, 145 playing with children, 160 dancing, 170 gardening, 250 running, roller-blading, cycling, and playing tennis or squash, and 260 swimming or cross-country skiing.

CHARACTERISTICS OF FATS

Fat is energy stored in deposits throughout the body (cheeks,, breasts, hips, abdomen, and so on) to be used in difficult times, such as prolonged fasting or physical effort carried out in the absence of sugars. It is the most calorific nutrient in nature, providing 9 calories per gram compared with 7 for alcohol and 4 for sugars and proteins. In addition, it performs the task of absorbing important liposoluble vitamins (A, D, E and K), and is the most important component of all the cellular membranes. First of all, it is necessary to distinguish between vegetable fat and animal fat. Various methods of classification exist, the most common being simple (glycerides) and complex (phospholipids) fats. The most important simple fats are triglycerides, consisting of glycerol and fatty acids, which we find in many foods. Triglycerides (which contain cholesterol) are the most important fats in the human body. Their concentration can be measured with a simple blood test.

At least 50 fatty acids are known, and these may– in turn be divided into saturated, trans or unsaturated fats (further classifiable in monounsaturated, i.e. short-chain, and polyunsaturated, i.e. long-chain,). Saturated fats, essentially of animal origin, are heavier, denser and less digestible. Unsaturated fats are, for the most part, derived from plants, and are more digestible and less dense. The division between animal and vegetable fats, however, is now somewhat obsolete: it is not true, in fact, that vegetable fats are all unsaturated, and therefore "good", and that animal fats all saturated, and therefore "bad" for our health. Extra-virgin olive oil, for example, although certainly of vegetable origin, contains 10% saturated fat, and, therefore, should not be consumed in excess. Another vegetable fat, coconut oil, contains 80% of saturated fats. Each time that we see the reassuring words "vegetable oils" or "vegetable fats" on the labels of packaged food, it is very likely that they derive from plants, but for the most part they are composed of saturated fats. On the contrary, many animal fats are not saturated. Those of salmon, for example, are almost 80% unsaturated, and also include fatty acids such as omega-3, important and useful for the body' s defences and for eyesight.

Daily calorie requirements depend on gender, height, weight and state of health. Obviously, only a nutrition expert, doctor or dietician can calculate the exact daily needs of a particular patient. In general, however, the daily diet should contain a level of fat equal to about 25% (up to a maximum of 30%) of the total calories. Monounsaturated and polyunsaturated fats should be taken in similar quantities (i.e. about 7-8% respectively), which brings the total unsaturated fats to approximately 14-16%, while saturated fats should be limited to a maximum of 7-8 %. Therefore, assuming that the overall percentage of fat is equal to approximately 25% of total calories, it can be divided into almost equal parts: 7-8% (almost one third of the total fat) saturated, 7-8% monounsaturated and 7-8% polyunsaturated. Of course, it is not necessary to check that the three types of fats are consumed in the exact proportions indicated for each meal, because what is important is variation, alternating the different sources of lipids throughout the course of the day. This indication is particularly important for those with a heart condition, vascular diseases or high rates of triglycerides and cholesterol in the blood. The remaining 1% of the 25% total fats is made up of trans fats, which are the most dangerous. Most foods contain all the fundamental types of fat – saturated, unsaturated (monounsaturated and polyunsaturated) and trans fats – but in varying proportions.

Saturated fats of animal origin are found in foods such as meat (beef, veal, lamb, pork, lard and the fatty part of chicken) and dairy products (butter, cream, whole milk and cheeses). Coconut oil and palm oil also have a high content of saturated fats. Trans fats come mainly from hydrogenated fats, unsaturated fats from vegetable oils, polyunsaturated fats from sunflower, corn and soya oils, and, finally, monounsaturated fats from colza and olive oil (those contained in colza are toxic).

Some unsaturated fats, called "essential fats", can only be assumed through diet (such as linoleic acid in olive oil), because our bodies are unable to produce them. Other unsaturated fats have proved to be important for the body's defences and to slow down degenerative diseases and ageing: this is the case, for example, with the omega-3 fatty acids, which can be found in salmon, eels and other oily fish. Omega-3 and omega-6 are polyunsaturated fatty acids possessing a double bond in position 3 (omega-3) and 6 (omega-6) of the chain that they form. Once introduced into our bodies, they are transformed into essential fatty acids. Omega-3, considered particularly important, is frequent in breast milk, plants and fish: the three most important types are EPA (eicosapentaenoic acid), DHA (docosahexaenoic), contained mainly in fish like salmon, and ALA (alpha-linolenic acid), which has a shorter molecule, contained in green leafy vegetables such as spinach, in vegetable oils (soya oil, colza oil and linseed oil) and especially in walnuts. DHA is the structural component of fundamental tissue such as the nervous system and the retina. In addition, it is important in the formation of substances suitable to repair oxidisation and damage caused by free radicals. Monounsaturated fats are relatively stable and have the double advantage of being easily conserved and resistant to high temperatures: the oils that contain predominantly monounsaturated fatty acids, such as olive oil and peanut oil, can therefore be used for frying.

On the contrary, a food to avoid, which is toxic especially for children, is colza oil, often used in certain sectors of the food industry. This oil contains high amounts of a monounsaturated acid – erucic acid – which has negative effects on the liver and on overall health. Other seed oils, such as those of corn, soy and sunflower, are rich in polyunsaturated fatty acids which, unfortunately, alter chemically when in contact with the light and air; for this reason they must be kept in well-sealed bottles or cans. Moreover, these oils destabilise at high temperatures, and therefore must never be used for frying. If well stored, they can be used raw as oils to dress salads, because they contain the same fatty acids – such as omega-3 and omega-6 – found in mackerel and in oily or semi-oily fish.

We must also be wary of hydrogenated fats produced through chemical processes specific to the food industry, that partially saturate many unsaturated fats. These processes cause the formation of trans fatty acids, which are highly atherogenic (i.e. they encourage fatty deposits in the arteries and consequently arteriosclerosis) and are much more dangerous than normal saturated fats. Saturated fats should be consumed in moderation as they contribute, together with cholesterol, to an increase in the risk of cardiovascular disease. If consumed in excess, they promote ageing of the blood vessels and arteriosclerosis. It is important that these do not exceed 78% of the daily calorie intake, but this figure must be further reduced for sufferers of vascular diseases and those wishing to lose weight. These fats are found in dairy products, fatty cheeses, red meat, offal (such as tripe), cold meats, fried foods (including fish), certain vegetable oils such as coconut and palm oil, ready meals with a high glycemic index, soft drinks, and industrially prepared fruit juices. It should be noted that out of all of these categories, butter is the most harmless, in spite of its calories (7.5 calories per gram), which make it unsuitable for dieters. There are some vegetable oils, in particular coconut and palm oil, which contain saturated fats that are highly atherogenic. These oils, often used by the food industry for snacks and other consumer foods, are denoted with the generic term of "vegetable oils"; this may engender the impression that they are harmless substances (also because they are often found in products for children), but in fact they encourage childhood obesity. The same may be said of margarines obtained from the plants used to create seed oils, which are wrongly perceived as being less dangerous than butter. Unfortunately, many of these margarines are subjected to industrial treatments which, while designed to maintain their consistency, transform them into fats that are much more dangerous than butter, i.e. trans fats.

Fats remain in the intestinal tube longer than carbohydrates, and are thus absorbed by the intestine; from here, they pass through the liver, where they can be used. If excessive fats are consumed, a small amount deposits in the muscles, while the majority are stored in the adipose tissue, thus increasing its mass. However, it is important to note that what is harmful to our health is not the saturated fat intake as such, but the excess of saturated fats in our diet. A certain amount of saturated fats are actually necessary for the body. The problem is that many saturated fats are consumed in our diet through foods that seem to be entirely innocuous: margarine, snacks, soft drinks, fruit juices, vegetable oils, ready meals, and so on.

## CHOLESTEROL

As with triglycerides, cholesterol is formed from fats circulating in the blood, the concentration of which can be measured with a simple blood test. It is a sterol whose name derives from the Greek *chole* (bile) and *stereos* (solid). It is whitish in colour and waxy in appearance. The human body synthesises all the cholesterol it requires, which is about 1.5 grams per day. The cholesterol found in blood, therefore, is for the most part of dietary origin, but it may also be produced in excess by the liver and the intestine. There are families in which some of their members, even if they follow a very strict diet, produce a very large quantity due to a genetic enzyme defect; this can lead to various problems in the long-term.

Cholesterol is essential for the production of cell membranes, for the formation of the embryo and foetus, for the production of many hormones produced by adrenal glands and the sexual glands (testosterone, aldosterone, cortisol, estradiol and so forth) and for the production of bile, which is necessary for the digestion of food fats in the small intestine. Its concentration and quality must, however, be optimal, otherwise in the long run it can cause vascular disease throughout the body. Its presence in the blood must not exceed 200 mg/dl: this fat tends to deposit on arterial walls, reducing their diameter, forming atheromas and reducing the blood circulation, with probable consequences for all of the body tissue and the possible occurrence of atherosclerosis, ischemia, strokes, and infarction (to the heart or brain).

Foods with a higher content of cholesterol are liver (chicken, pork and veal), tripe, sweetbreads, eggs, butter and, among cheeses, mascarpone, Swiss emmenthal, provolone and Dutch gouda. Foods with a slightly lower content than the above are bacon, frankfurters, sausage, shellfish, crustaceans, and eels. Of course, eating foods with a high content of saturated fats and cholesterol – such as meat, poultry, shellfish and dairy products, even low-fat versions – can raise our cholesterol level; smoking too increases the circulation of cholesterol in our blood. A simple reduction of 5% in the saturated fat intake in our diet (substituting it with other polyunsaturates) can have a substantial impact on the total level of cholesterol in our blood, leading to a 10-15 % reduction in the risk of developing heart and vascular disease.

The total cholesterol in the blood is an interesting indicator. However, there are several types of cholesterol and some of them have an antagonistic effect: there is not only a cholesterol that is "bad" for our health, there is also a "good" one. Cholesterol and fatty acids join the blood proteins, creating a particular class of substances called "lipoproteins", which, depending on their density, are divided into High Density Lipoproteins (HDL), Low Density Lipoproteins (LDL), and Very Low Density Lipoproteins (VLDL). Not all cholesterol fractions circulating in the blood are dangerous: HDL can remove cholesterol from atheromas on the arteries, cleansing them from the inside and keeping the blood vessels elastic . Sometimes, therefore, problems arise not so much due to the presence of a high percentage of cholesterol in the blood, but due the fact that its HDL level is too low. In a healthy person, HDL must be present in levels above 45 mg/dl. Unsaturated fats of vegetable origin and those derived from fish stimulate the synthesis of HDL and thus exert a preventative action against possible vascular damage. The percentage of HDL is increased also by physical exercise and through the moderate consumption of red wine. That is why it is not sufficient just to measure the level of cholesterol in the blood, but it is necessary to carry out a lipid profile, an examination that identifies the percentage value of lipoproteins present in cholesterol. The World Health Organisation (WHO) recommends that total blood cholesterol levels should be lower than 200 mg/dl and that the ratio of total cholesterol/HDL should not be greater than 5 for men and 4.5 for women. Excess cholesterol represents one of the main causes of cardiovascular diseases, which kill more than 17 million people each year. Multiple studies carried out over decades have shown a direct proportionality between the total cholesterol and the risk of cardiovascular mortality (thrombosis, heart attack and atherosclerosis), especially for cholesterol levels higher than 220 mg/dl and, in particular, when the proportion of LDL is high. Full fat cow's milk, coconut and palm oils, meat, fish, shellfish and industrial margarines are the strongest stimuli for the production of LDL. Some studies have proved that in populations with particularly high cholesterol levels in the blood (due to diet, socio-economic status and metabolic diseases) there is a direct relationship between these factors and the occurrence of ischemic cardiac diseases such as angina, heart attack, strokes, coronary heart disease and similar pathologies. In the United States, however, the percentage of deaths from heart attack is much higher than that for Italy and France, even if the average level of cholesterol in the blood of Americans is less than that of the Italians and even lower than that of the French. This complicates things further, leading experts to favour a less simplistic view, according to which cholesterol, if not aided by other factors related to lifestyle and nutrition, does not in itself cause vascular disease. Moreover, populations that eat almost exclusively animal products rich in cholesterol such as the Masai (dairy products) and the Inuit (seal fat) have lower cholesterol levels than the inhabitants of Europe and North America. High cholesterol, therefore, may not be attributed solely to a diet rich in cholesterol, as might be imagined at first glance. Moreover, genetics also play their part. In some inhabitants of Limone sul Garda, for example, a genetic factor was discovered that causes a particular variation, corresponding to a very low risk of developing heart vascular disease: such a mutation, in fact, greatly increases the efficiency of HDL, both as a cleaner of the arteries and as a factor in prevention. There is also a strong correlation between stress and cholesterol levels: the proportion of cholesterol in the blood rises in proportion to an increase in stress hormones (adrenaline and cortisol). In particular, cortisol inhibits the metabolism of LDL by the liver. Today, therefore, it is fairly safe to say that there is a definite relationship between stress and "bad" cholesterol in the blood, based on which, the lower the stress, the higher the level of "good" cholesterol .

PHYTOSTEROLS

Phytosterols (beta-sitosterosl, phytosterols and the like) are vegetable lipid substances that are chemically very similar to animal cholesterol. Basically, we could say that they constitute a sort of "vegetable cholesterol". They are found in nuts, seeds and in soy, but assume a particular concentration in cold-pressed oils such as soybean oil, which is widely used in the food industry to produce ready meals, margarines and fats: these often state that they are "cholesterol free" on the label, a declaration that is illusory both for vegetarians and those following "DIY" diets.

Unfortunately, these substances are, in fact, potentially dangerous: sitosterols (also used as drugs in prostatic hyperplasia), for example, increase the incidence of coronary heart disease and vascular diseases.

## TRIGLYCERIDES

Triglycerides (TG) belong to the family of glycerides and are glycerol esters formed from three medium or long chain fatty acids. They cannot cross the cell membranes, but some enzymes called "lipases" can reduce them to fatty acids and glycerol, causing lipolysis and, therefore, the intracellular passage of these constituent elements.

TGs make up the majority of fats deposited in the adipose tissue and a significant proportion of that circulating in the blood. These too derive essentially from diet, but may also be formed to a small extent by the liver. As with cholesterol, there are families in which some members, if not all, produce an abundance of TGs, despite not introducing them in excess in their diet. The maximum level allowed for TGs is 150 mg/dl. An unbalanced diet and diabetes encourages an increase in TGs in the blood, leading to vascular diseases, as is the case with dangerously high cholesterol.

Unlike for carbohydrates, the breakdown of fats is not complete, and therefore numerous waste substances are formed, such as ketone bodies which, when present in excessive quantities, are in part released in the urine or breath (acetone in children). There is often a relationship between a simultaneous increase in cholesterol and TG in the blood, on the one hand, and an increasing incidence of arteriosclerosis, on the other.

## LECITHINS

Among complex fats, lecithins are particularly important. They can be found in egg yolk and in plants (for example soybeans, peanuts, oats, and so on). Lecithins, from the Greek *lekithos* (egg yolk), are a group of yellowy to dark brown substances, some solid and others fluid. They are a mixture of different fatty substances (fatty acids, glycerols, triglycerides and phospholipids with the addition of choline and phosphoric acid), of which phospholipids are the most important component. Lecithins are emulsifiers, naturally classifiable somewhere between water and fatty substances, allowing them to blend elements which otherwise would be difficult to mix. They are essential in the formation of cell membranes. Moreover, they also have the ability to agglutinate, and are natural antagonists of cholesterol. In the nutritional field, they are mixed with yoghurt, honey, fruits, soups and the like, or can be found in bars. Being formed for the most part by linoleic acid, they are able to counteract the formation of gallstones and can be used to combat liver diseases and prevent both degenerative alteration of blood vessels and deposits of grease in the cardiovascular system; in addition, under certain conditions, they can help to improve the elasticity of blood vessels and prevent deposit of cholesterol on artery walls. They are often used in the food industry as emulsifiers to produce chocolate, sweets, chewing gum, ready meals, bakery products, cheeses, meat-based dishes, and more. Their emulsifying properties, however, are increased by the use of other fats, and therefore it is not known with certainty whether their protective effects persist. Ultimately, we must distinguish between the pure chemical substance and that contained in natural food: they are two different things, because many interactions between chemical substances and food products are not yet known. In general, it is more appropriate and more prudent to consume a certain substance by eating it directly as a food rather than as an industrial chemical mix.

FAT, EXCESSIVE WEIGHT AND OBESITY

Fat is bad. No one likes fat. Fat is a no go. It is not only a question of aesthetics. Unfortunately, it has been scientifically proven that too much fat shortens life, and, above all, makes it more troublesome. Among our friends, family and children, we are increasingly witnessing more and more cases of weight gain and obesity. In time, this will become a social "weight" that will be difficult to bear. Taking care of our diet is the first way to fight this condition, and to prevent it without compromising on taste and the pleasure of eating.

First of all, let's try to define excessive weight and obesity more clearly. Rather simplistically, someone may be defined as obese if he or she weighs 25% more than a hypothetical twin of the same height and of normal weight. For example, if we take two 6 foot twins, the normal one would weigh 12 stone (75 kg) and the obese one 16 (100 kg).

To be more precise, an obese individual has 25% more body fat than is considered normal for his or her gender and age. But how do we know if our weight is normal? The calculation most widely in use today is the Body Mass Index (BMI).

This index is obtained by dividing the weight in kilograms by the square of the height expressed in metres, i.e.:

$$\frac{\text{Weight in kilograms}}{\text{height in metres x height in metres}} = \text{BMI}$$

It follows that, depending on the value of the BMI, each of us may be considered underweight, of normal weight, overweight, or obese, regardless of whether we are male or female.

A BMI of less than 18.5 means being underweight
A BMI of between 18.5 and 24.9 means being of normal weight
A BMI of between 25 and 29.9 means being overweight
A BMI of between 30 and 34.9 means class I obesity
A BMI of between 35 and 39.9 means class II obesity
A BMI of between 40 and 45 means class III obesity
A BMI of between 46 and 50 means class I severe obesity
A BMI of between 51 and 55 means class II severe obesity
A BMI of between 51 and 55 means class III severe obesity

It is believed that normal weight corresponds to a BMI of less than 23 for women and less than 25 for men. While these figures are valid for Caucasian white people, several studies have demonstrated that Asians develop diseases with a BMI even lower than those usually considered normal. In Japan, for example, individuals are considered obese with a BMI greater than 25 and in China with a BMI greater than 28.

The risk of mortality is lower in non-smokers and in those who have a BMI between 20 and 25; it increases proportionally as the BMI increases.

Globally, obesity is the fifth greatest risk for mortality, causing the death of approximately 3 million people each year, including a million in Europe and half a million in the United States of America. Obesity is just as dangerous to our health as smoking too many cigarettes. What is more, we have seen that cigarette smoking is capable of raising the content of some fats in the blood, such as cholesterol. In the case of females, if the BMI is greater than 32, the risk of mortality doubles within 15 years. It has been estimated that a BMI greater than 30 reduces life by 67 years; but above all, it changes the quality of life for the last 20 or 30 years. A simple method to calculate the danger of being overweight is to measure the abdominal circumference at navel height with a tape measure. If it is more than 89cm for a woman and 102 cm for a man, the risk that being overweight will create health complications is high.

There is no absolute value to indicate obesity in children and adolescents, because the weight of a baby depends on age, type of growth and gender. The method used to evaluate obesity is similar to that used to analyse growth: paediatricians make calculations according to average growth curves, which are highly variable from one subject to the next because family factors are so very different. In any case, these curves are still useful because they provide a clear idea on how growth is proceeding from one year to the next, and in particular on whether it has been excessive or insufficient over the last 12 months, according to statistical parameters generated on the basis of the characteristics of that individual child. Similarly, in the assessment of obesity a single weight can be considered normal or abnormal, depending on the height of the child and his or her age; what counts is the variation in weight from one year to the next. If we wish to establish a general criterion, we can say that, taking a group of average children as reference, a child is considered obese if his or her level of growth considerably exceeds this average.

However, it is not possible to make a precise diagnosis of obesity based solely on the BMI, because this index does not take into consideration differences in muscle mass, i.e. lean and fat mass, namely the actual adipose tissue of the subject in question. Indeed, taking two people who both weigh 16 stone (100 kg), one may have 10% more fat than a normal person, and the other 60% more; in this case, despite having the same weight, the difference in their appearance will be considerable. The first will probably be an athlete used to strenuous exercise, and hence with a large lean muscle mass, while the second may never have worked out in a gym, and his or her fat will be plentiful due to a low muscle mass. To accurately measure the ratio between the two masses, special electrical bio-impedance technology used by medical specialists and dieticians, or other specialist devices, is required.

In the case of the overweight or obese, excessive pounds can be more or less dangerous for our health, depending on where they accumulate. In particular, if the fat deposits in the lower parts of the body (hips, thighs, buttocks and belly below the navel), this type of obesity is called pear-shaped or peripheral or ginecoide, a phenomenon that can cause arthritis of the hip or knee, especially in females, among whom it is most frequent. If, on the other hand, the fat accumulates in the upper parts of the body (neck, shoulders and belly above the navel), this is referred to as apple-shaped or central or android. This type of obesity is more common among males and can lead to cardiovascular disease (strokes and heart attacks), type 2 diabetes (due to an insulin dysfunction), gout, hypertension, high cholesterol and respiratory insufficiency.

## EXCESS WEIGHT AND OBESITY IN THE WORLD

According to the World Health Organisation (WHO), 12% of the world's population (half a billion people) is considered obese. Obesity increases with age, especially after 45-50 years, and is certainly more frequent in women.

Since average life expectancy is on the up, today this pathology is also increasing, particularly in rich Western countries: the highest rates occur in the Americas (26% of the adult population), compared with a percentage of 3% – the lowest in the world – in southeast Asia. Obesity, moreover, is also becoming increasingly frequent in developing countries, although it remains relatively low in Sahel countries (Sub-Saharan Africa). The main cause of this increase is the change, inspired by the Anglo-Saxon model, that has occurred in recent years in diet and lifestyle, characterised by a high protein and high sugar diet based on red meats, industrially prepared foods, ready meals and sugary drinks.

Throughout Europe, including the Mediterranean and the east, obesity is increasing at breakneck speed, in particular among young people: there are more and more cases recorded of children and adolescents who, at least in 60% of cases, inevitably carry this condition with them into adulthood. Of approximately 45 million children under 5 years of age who are overweight, 35 million of them live in developing countries. Among children, excessive weight is greater in males, and the age-group most affected is between 11 and 12 years old. Poor nutrition and lack of exercise are the bases of childhood obesity, but we must not underestimate hormonal problems and pharmacological therapies. Today, for example, it is well known that the latest generation anti-psychotic drugs may encourage both type 2 diabetes and obesity, right from childhood.

## CAUSES OF EXCESSIVE WEIGHT AND OBESITY

The word "obesity" comes from the Latin *obesitas*, a term derived from *obesus*, which means "fat, big". The condition should be regarded as a fully-fledged, chronic disease caused by a variety of concomitant factors that interact with each other without excluding one other.

The main causes are:
1) Genetic factors and family members with a constitutional predisposition
2) Poor diet
3) Sedentary lifestyle
4) Metabolic Diseases

1) There exists a genetic predisposition to obesity. The risk of becoming obese if one parent is already obese is 50%, and this rises to 80-90% if both are obese. However, the predisposition may be linked to maladjusted cerebral circuits that control hunger or the fact that particular automatic behavioural traits are acquired from the family context.

In some populations – such as some peoples of Polynesia and the desert-inhabiting Pima Indians – obesity is particularly common. These hereditary tendencies typical of circumscribed areas may be the result of genetic selection in a population: in ecosystems in which the condition of hunger often exists, obese individuals may survive better due to their reserves of fat. They are believed to have a "saver" gene that allows them to better store fat in deposits even in times of dearth, but that in case of normal nutrition conditions makes them put on weight. There are also subjects who produce excess fats, for example cholesterol or triglycerides, and who, while following very restrictive diets, continue to have higher than average levels of fats in the blood due to an abnormal overproduction by the liver, often due to family reasons.

2) Nutrition, one of the cornerstones of the therapy against obesity, is linked to psychological, cultural, social and hormonal factors that must be considered together.

The calorie intake in the modern diet has increased, not only due to fats, but, above all, because of the increase in the consumption of sugars. This is particularly serious among young people and children, due to the consumption of energy drinks, soft drinks and snacks. A further critical factor is represented by the success of fast food chains, with their high-calorie fried meals. In the United States, the food industry lobby has succeeded in obtaining subsidies paid by the government for the cultivation of corn, soybeans, wheat and rice, widely used at low cost on an industrial level and in battery farming of livestock; however, consumer prices for the foods that would be more suitable to fighting obesity, i.e. fruit and vegetables, remain very high. The result is that a hamburger in a bun has a relatively low cost, while a peach has a high consumer cost, in spite of the fact that the producers of fruit and vegetables obtain almost no benefit from this high price. Burning off a hamburger from an industrial food production line takes 4 hours of continuous running, an extremely difficult task, while 11 lb (5 kg) of fruit equate to just 3 1/2 oz (100 g) of biscuits produced by an industrial multinational.

Added to this is the increase, among the world's youth, in the use of alcohol and spirits, which provide a significant calorie intake without contributing any nutrients and, in fact, slowing down the metabolism. It is estimated that non-drinkers have two to three times lower abdominal fat deposits than drinkers.

Local culture has a strong influence on the acceptance of obesity and on food rhythms, the latter being very fast-paced in the West, encouraging people to rapidly devour a large quantity of high-calorie foods, a situation that often leads to obesity. There are also cultures with slower rhythms, but in which "fat is beautiful" because the idea of chubbiness signifies wealth and health. This is the case for poor environments or ones which have recently emerged from a period of dearth. In the West, it has been demonstrated that women of a higher social class are less likely to be obese than those from poorer social classes, because they can take better care of themselves and dedicate more time to their own bodies, in addition to eating a healthier diet. Instead, in some African societies, for example, where hunger is common, the exact opposite occurs.

In central Africa, when the AIDS epidemic struck in the early 1980s, it was first called the "disease of the thin", because this immunodeficiency syndrome, i.e. a state in which the immune system's ability to fight infectious disease is compromised or entirely absent, causes the sufferer to progressively waste away. As a result, in these areas overweight female figures have become a very reassuring sign, indicating that the subject is not affected by the "disease of the thin".

3) We cannot ignore the importance of physical exercise in preventing weight loss leading to the loss of lean mass rather than fat mass. In the Western world, physically demanding work has significantly reduced and, therefore, we should be eating less. Only those who play sport can afford to eat a little more, but unfortunately, after a certain age many professionals continue to eat a lot without, however, training with the same intensity; becoming overweight is a therefore natural consequence.

It is estimated that 60% of the world's population does not perform sufficient physical activity. Household appliances, cars and means of communication, such as televisions, PCs, tablets, and so on, have increased exponentially. In particular, children's lifestyles have changed much over the past 40 years. Once children would play in groups, outside in the open air, for long periods of the day. Today, instead, they stay indoors, either at home or at school, for hours on end, often "glued" to the computer.

Society has changed considerably, and this will inevitably result in an increase in obesity. If we simply walked more and did sports and physical exercise at least three times a week – never immediately after meals – we could mobilise our reserves of fat. Physical activity is always necessary, and not just for losing weight. Our overall health significantly improves, we socialise more, we learn new things, and we discover new opportunities through the relationships that develop alongside such activities.

In any case, it is wise to use some common sense. Running a marathon without eating means losing lean body mass (muscle proteins) and liver glycogen (the store of carbohydrates in the liver), and this is profoundly wrong. Fortunately, someone wishing to lose weight is unlikely to run a 20 mile marathon with no training.

In general, physical effort should be quite heavy; only in this way can the body concentrate on recovering its resources after the sporting activity has finished, without feeling the pangs of hunger. A slight physical effort, such as a short walk in the mountains, on the other hand, stimulates the body to feel the need to recover energy through eating. The efforts made, therefore, must be sufficiently intense not to stimulate the appetite once the activity is finished, but rather the need for rest or even sleep.

4) Until recently, obesity was considered a problem linked exclusively with over eating, but today we know that there are also various hormonal dysfunctions (related to the thyroidal, adrenal and pituitary glands, etc.) that, in isolation, can also cause at least a certain degree of obesity: some obese people eat exactly the same as others, but their bodies do not burn the calories in the normal way and so they accumulate and transform them into fatty substances. There are also many psychological forms, such as night eating syndrome or uncontrolled eating disorders, which obviously lead to weight gain.

Moreover, there are further more minor factors, both hypothetical and proven, that can complicate matters. It should not be ignored, for example, that some environmental pollutants can interfere with hormonal systems, as can also the use of pharmaceutical drugs, especially cortisones, insulin, oestrogen and progestogens used in hormonal treatments or as contraceptives, and medications for psychological problems, in particular tranquillisers, sleeping pills and anti-depressants.

We also know that, when people stop smoking, within a short space of time they begin to put on weight. In women, an increase in weight can perhaps be caused by the fact that pregnancies now occur later than in the past and, following childbirth, a woman is not always able to return to her previous pre-pregnancy weight.

Finally, for many years we have known that the gut flora of the obese is different from that of those of normal weight. Whether this, however, is a consequence of obesity or a further contributing factor, has yet to been ascertained. Should a causal link be true, this could be explained by the fact that bacteria in the gut may or may not encourage the absorption of certain energetic nutrients.

Once medical investigation has excluded the possibility of hormonal alterations, the winning strategy should consist of a three-pronged approach to obesity, including diet, a healthy psychological approach to lifestyle and physical exercise. One of these three actions is not sufficient to reduce weight in the obese, in the absence of the other two. An exclusively dietary approach would be particularly damaging, as the risk would be to lose weight in water and lean mass rather than in fat mass, and to put the weight straight back on following the end of the diet.

In order to treat the condition of obesity, it is vital for patients to realise, first of all, that there is a problem, and that the situation will lead to a series of complications in the future. Only in this way will they become truly aware of their condition, and take full responsibility for it, so as to become the real driving force behind the therapy. Not being convinced about the condition means the therapy cannot be successful. It is important, therefore, not to follow diets read in books, or seen on television, or recommended by a friend with the same problem. People suffering from obesity must contact a specialised professional.

Unfortunately, there are no medicines nor miracle diets. Sudden weight loss obtained by the wrong practices leads to the loss of lean rather than fat mass, and this may have serious repercussions on the patient's health, in the short or medium term.

OBESITY AS A CAUSE OF DISEASE

Obesity can cause many types of diseases in different parts of the body. It often goes hand in hand with high blood pressure, increased cholesterol and triglyceride levels in the blood, and type 2 diabetes, creating further complications in all these pathologies.

On a cardiological level, it can lead to angina and heart attacks, but also hypertension, vascular disease and thrombosis.

On a respiratory level, it can cause asthma and nocturnal apnea, and can increase the probability of complications during general anaesthesia.

On an endocrinological level, it can lead to diabetes and polycystic ovarian disease, as well as gynecomastia, infertility and menstrual disorders.

On a gastroenterological level, it can cause gall stones, liver disease and gastroesophageal reflux (hiatus hernia).

On a dermatological level, it can cause stretch marks and hirsutism.

On a neurological level, it can encourage migraine, multiple sclerosis and carpal tunnel syndrome.

On an oncological level, it can lead to the onset of breast, gastrointestinal, ovarian, prostate, kidney and blood cancer (myeloma and lymphoma).

On a rheumatological and orthopaedic level, it can contribute to the onset of gout, rheumatism, arthritis, back pain, osteoporosis, and scoliosis.

On a urological level, it can encourage hypogonadism, renal insufficiency, erectile dysfunction and urinary incontinence.

Finally, obesity can indirectly lead to low self-esteem, depression, social isolation, lack of integration in the workplace, and relationship problems.

THE MEDITERRANEAN DIET

The Mediterranean diet, awarded Unesco World Heritage status, today represents an effective dietary bulwark against the chronic diseases of the elderly and for the prevention and treatment of metabolic diseases related to diabetes, hyperlipidaemia, vascular disease, heart disease and cancer, in particular of the gastrointestinal tract.

This low-fat diet mainly contains safe fats, such as those obtained from plants, e.g. extra virgin olive oil, and fish.

Most of its calories come from complex carbohydrates such as pasta, bread and wholegrain rices, which are assisted by a rich set of fibres; these include fresh fruit, seasonal vegetables and pulses, that also provide useful vitamins and antioxidants.

In particular, calories deriving from fats should be limited to no more than 30% of the total, two-thirds of which from extra-virgin olive oil and/or fish, and only a third from saturated fat, i.e. cheeses and meats. It is necessary to limit the intake of cholesterol in food, and it is advisable to consume no more than a small glass of wine, preferably red, with each meal.

We must also reduce salt to no more than 3 grams per day. Since this dosage is generally exceeded in industrial packaged foods, the ideal would be to use only natural sea salt and never refined salt.

An interesting fact: the term "Mediterranean diet" was coined in 1959 by two American researchers, Ancel and Margaret Keys, who lived in Pioppi, near Pollica, in the province of Salerno, for more than twenty years, studying the life conditions of the inhabitants of the Cilento region. The conclusion they reached was that, to stay in good health, it is necessary to limit saturated fats from meats, cold cuts, baked goods and dairy products, to use extra-virgin olive oil, to avoid refined salt and sugar, and, finally, to exercise regularly.

TIPS FOR A HEALTHY DIET

Following a diet is always complicated, but you must begin by accepting that slimming down and improving our health should not be a sacrifice. To this end, it is important to eat a little of all food types, rationing, in most cases, the quantity rather than the quality. It is also necessary to set specific objectives, and to achieve them one at a time. It is essential to learn how to be in control of your environment, i.e. to be able to reduce the stimuli of an unhealthy diet and to share this attitude with other members of the family.

Every diet requires sacrifices, but some small gratification is also required: this must be calculated, and then burned off through physical exercise. Fish must not be consumed fried: better baked, barbecued, steamed, stewed, or, if possible and if it is well sourced and safe, raw. Meat must be lean and white (poultry, game), yoghurt must be natural and low-fat, cereals should be wholegrain and complex.

It is therefore worth following the Mediterranean diet as closely as possible. Your must set aside the idea that to lose weight it is sufficient not to eat fatty foods: excess sugars also transform into fat, and physical exercise is a must. Ideally, education on how to adopt a healthy diet should start at school and in the home. This would also provide effective prevention some 30-40 years on, with a considerable impact on our society and economy. After all, children follow their parents' example, and they also learn from what they find on offer at school and at home.

Parents are often concerned when their child doesn't eat much; in reality, the most serious problems occur when, on the contrary, the child eats too much. Moreover, often they not only eat too much compared to the physical activity they perform; they also eat badly and in an unbalanced manner – which is even worse – by consuming too many high-calorie foods and soft drinks, strongly promoted by the food industry and readily available everywhere (even in hospitals, in the subway and at school, through vending machines).

A simple sandwich is certainly nutritious, but its calorie content may be even higher than that of a meal: it depends on what it contains, and on how you eat it. In the worst case, it will have a high salt and fat content, and will be very low in fibre. It would be more advisable to use wholemeal bread and, to increase the amount of fibre, to add vegetables (courgettes, aubergines and the like), preferably grilled rather than preserved in oil. Instead of cold cuts (which are red meat!), it is preferable to fill sandwiches with turkey, chicken, tuna, mozzarella and tomatoes. Furthermore, you should never add butter, ketchup or mayonnaise. When having a sandwich, which should never be very large, it is important to eat it in small bites, and to chew it well, dedicating time to this activity; the meal should be eaten in at least 20 minutes. While eating a sandwich you should not do anything else: do not drive, walk, or work at the computer. Plan your shopping ahead with a detailed list, and do not be enticed by the foods on display, either in terms of appearance or cost; you must learn to stick to what's on the list. Devote time to doing the shopping. Learn to be patient and to read and understand the labels (bring the right glasses!), so as to be able to make informed choices. Producers are obliged by law to print them, and they often use small print because they do not want you to read them! Only buy small portions, even if they are proportionally more expensive, and limit the supplies at home. The refrigerator should never be full. Learn not to throw food away and not to let it expire: this is easier if the refrigerator is not full. And the food will keep better if there is space between one item and another, even in the freezer. You should only buy food with a low energy index and food that should be in some way prepared: never buy ready or frozen meals, and try to reduce consumption of these products to a minimum. To lose weight and stay healthy, it is also important to know how to divide up meals. Never taste food while you are preparing it. Don't go out to restaurants too often, or frequent only well-known establishments, where you know what happens in the kitchen. It is a good rule to sit at the table and eat without haste, breathing deeply and chewing every bite well. Never eat standing up or in front of the television; instead, use meals as occasions for conviviality and interaction. It is important to only bring to the dining table what you have previously decided to eat, and nothing more. Remove all foods that can lead you into temptation, both from the table and from the refrigerator. Never drink industrially produced sugary, fizzy or energy drinks at the dining table.

Beer and wine should be consumed in moderation, but a glass of natural red wine at each meal is not only allowed, but has been scientifically demonstrated to be healthy too.

We must not consume too much sugar at night, because at the end of the day the metabolism slows down and digestion becomes more difficult. At dinnertime, it is advisable to eat vegetables, protein and fibre.

To lose weight, it is better to eat proteins rather than sugar, because a meal containing proteins speeds up the metabolism more than one with sugars.

Finally, it is very important to drink lots of still rather than sparkling water: ideally 2 or 3 litres per day, especially in the summer. During the hot season, we lose weight because the body loses water through perspiration. As a result, the body dehydrates and the metabolism slows down, thus consuming less fat. Water can never make you fat. It is satisfying, facilitates intestinal motility and renal purification, and fights the development of kidney and gall stones. Drinking lots of water is important to stay young.

LIGHT, LOW FAT STARTERS. OR, PERHAPS, EVEN COMPLETELY FAT FREE. WITH STEAMING OR GRILLING, CRUDITÉES AND SMOOTHIES. WHY? TO REDUCE CALORIES WITHOUT GIVING UP ON TASTE, AND ALL TO THE BENEFIT OF OUR HEALTH!

Food is more than it seems. It is sustenance, a moment of peace, an opportunity to recharge our batteries, a gratifying moment of our day. And then there's comfort food, to which we turn as a response to emotional stress. Food gives us the strength we need, and so we should take a moment to learn what we should and shouldn't eat. Certain foods can also be a health hazard, and

therefore we must be ready to take onboard any specific dietary needs we may have. We should consider food as an ally for our wellbeing; friends with which to calculate our calorie intake, so as to understand when we have gone overboard. Food is not our enemy. It is what we see in food that can lead us astray!

If we really want to loose a few pounds, have regular triglyceride and cholesterol levels, and – why not? – feel ever so slightly superior before those appetizing but high calorie foods, we should arm ourselves with the necessary tools to conquer our gluttony. It is possible to turn low calorie foods into flavorsome and attractive dishes. Whether savouring a simple appetiser or a starter, what counts is the ability to be gratified and energised by the food we eat. Starters, the function of which is to introduce us to a tasty meal, are often a collection of sauces, fats and proteins. What we must learn to do is consider the amount of calories we need in a day and how many constitute our regular diet, and then act accordingly. We can devise intriguing starters, to end the day and start the evening in a worthy fashion, with light, creamy, colourful and aromatic dishes. Simply replace oil with spices, butter with alternative cooking

# STARTERS

techniques, and we will see the calorie content of our diet reduce, just like our waistline!

Of course, we need to change our approach to flavor. But let's try to imagine an extra light world in which fats are reduced to a minimum, giving precedence to those rich in omega-3 or omega-6. It is worth a try, to discover just how precious unsaturated fats are in the fight against the damaged caused by ageing, damage that saturated fats can accelerate. If you are reading these words, it is because you are seeking an alternative form of nutrition, so sit back and enjoy fresh vegetable smoothies, rice stuffed leek parcels, tasty salads, inviting cream sauces, appetizing salmon tartares, juicy fruits, and flavorsome but ultra light cold cuts!

# LAYERED VEGETABLE SMOOTHIE

*Basil is a herb that contains several trace elements (potassium, phosphorus, magnesium and zinc), vitamins A, C, E and from the B complex, and many amino acids (tryptophan, lysine, leucine, arginine and alanine). It was once used to cure nervous conditions and to increase milk production in young mothers. It is an excellent digestive, stimulates the appetite and helps relieve psychological distress such as anxiety and insomnia.*

EASY

**4 servings**
Preparation time: **15 minutes**
Calories per serving: **80**

3/4 cup (200 g) low-fat
yoghurt
10 1/2 oz. (300 g) tomatoes
7 oz. (200 g) cucumber
1 bunch fresh herbs
(mint and basil)
1 tsp (2 g) dry coriander
1 tsp (2 g) cumin
1 tbsp (5 g) cardamom pods
8 black olives
Pepper

1. Wash, slice, seed and peel the tomatoes, draining the excess liquid through a strainer. Trim, wash and dice the cucumber.

2. With a mincing knife or blender, mince the herbs and spices, except the basil which will be used as a garnish.

3. Blend the tomatoes and cucumber separately and pour the mixtures into two separate bowls. Add the chopped mint to the cucumber and the chopped coriander to the tomato.

4. Mix the chopped cumin and cardamom into the yoghurt.

5. Take four Martini glasses, place a spoon inside each, then gently pour in the tomato puree followed by the cucumber and the yoghurt. In this way, the ingredients will not mix together, creating three separate coloured layers.

6. Skewer two olives with a toothpick and place them on each glass. Sprinkle with pepper and garnish with basil leaves. Serve at room temperature.

# TOFU AND SUNFLOWER SEED SALAD

*Sunflower seeds are the oilseeds lowest in calories, despite containing essential fatty acids such as folic and linoleic acid (omega-6). In addition to B complex vitamins (especially vitamin B12, a useful supplement for vegetarian and vegan diets), they contain vitamins A, D and E, as well as being an excellent source of iron, copper, zinc and magnesium. In particular, they help lower the level of cholesterol in the blood and prevent heart and blood vessel diseases.*

EASY

**4 servings**
Preparation time: **10 minutes**
Calories per serving: **150**

7 oz. (200 g) salad leaves
2 tbsp (20 g) sunflower seeds
3/4 oz. (20 g) cranberries
3 1/2 oz. (100 g) tofu
1 bunch parsley
Salt
Pepper
Balsamic vinegar (optional)
1 lemon (optional)

*1.* Wash the parsley, then remove the stems and mince the leaves.

*2.* Clean, wash, dry and roughly chop the salad.

*3.* In a non-stick pan, toast the sunflower seeds for a few minutes to release their fat and make them easier to digest.

*4.* Place the salad, cranberries and sunflower seeds in a salad bowl. Drain and chop the tofu, and add it to the salad. If you prefer, you can first sautée the tofu in a non-stick pan for a few minutes. Mix the ingredients and add the chopped parsley.

*5.* Sprinkle with salt and pepper. If you like, you can add a few drops of balsamic vinegar and decorate with freshly cut lemon slices, then serve.

# LEEK AND RICOTTA FLAN

*Leek, a valid substitute for onion, has long been known for its beneficial properties. Low in calories and rich in vitamins A and C, it also contains many minerals, including calcium, potassium and phosphorus. It is good for the nervous system, and is also a mild laxative and purifying agent, thus serving as a useful aid in slimming diets.*

**EASY**

**4 servings**
Preparation time: **15-20 minutes**
Cooking time: **20-30 minutes**
Calories per serving: **219**

4 leeks
7 oz. (200 g) fresh ricotta cheese
1 tsp cornflour
3/4 cup (200 g) soy cream
Nutmeg to taste
Oil and butter to grease the moulds
Salt
Pepper

1. Preheat the oven to 320° F (160° C).

2. Wash and trim the leeks, then cut them in half and place them in a steamer basket. Cook to obtain the desired consistency (approximately 15-20 minutes).

3. Finely chop the cooked leeks, keeping a few leaves, cut into strips, as garnish. Pour the mixture into a bowl, and add the ricotta cheese, soy cream and cornflour. Mix and sprinkle with nutmeg, salt and pepper. Stir until all the ingredients are well mixed.

4. Grease four single-portion moulds and pour in the mixture. Place them in a baking dish about one-third filled with water and oven cook them in the bain-marie for about 20-30 minutes. Place a kitchen cloth under the moulds to stop the boiling water from toppling them over while cooking.

5. Once cooked, remove the moulds from the oven and leave to rest for a few minutes. Turn the flans out and serve garnished with strips of steamed leeks.

# COURGETTE ROLL

*Courgettes are easy to digest, high in water (which makes up 94% of their weight) and low in calories. Moreover, they are rich in minerals (potassium, iron, calcium and phosphorus), vitamins (A, C, B1 and B2) and antioxidant bioflavonoids, such as lutein and zeaxanthin, which are useful anti-ageing substances not commonly found in the food we eat (which is why they are used in many supplements). Consequently, courgettes are ideal in diets and are believed to be an excellent anti-ageing food. Furthermore, they boast laxative, purifying and diuretic properties.*

MEDIUM

**4 servings**
Preparation time: **20 minutes**
Cooking time: **15 minutes**
Resting time: **2 hours**
Calories per serving: **210**

**For the roll:**
2 green courgettes, large
2 potatoes
1 mozzarella
(approximately 3 1/2 oz./100 g)
7 oz. (200 g) fresh ricotta
Salt
Pepper

**For the garnish:**
1 baby lettuce head
4 cherry tomatoes
1 sprig fresh oregano
1 tbsp apple vinegar (optional)

1. Trim and wash the courgettes. Then, using a potato peeler, slice them into long, thin strips.

2. Steam the whole potatoes for about 15 minutes. Once cooked, allow them to cool before peeling and dicing them. Dice the mozzarella cheese.

3. Place the potatoes and mozzarella into a bowl and mix in the ricotta. Add salt and pepper to taste.

4. Clean, wash and dry the lettuce leaves and oregano, then set them aside, wrapping the lettuce in a damp cloth. Wash the tomatoes.

5. Put a sheet of cling film on a chopping board and place the courgette strips in a line.

6. Pour the mixture on top of the courgettes, then roll them on themselves lengthwise using the cling film. Place the roll in the refrigerator for about 2 hours, to enable the ingredients to blend and the mixture to set. Remove the cling film and cut the roll into slices.

7. At the time of serving, place the slices on a bed of salad and decorate with freshly cut tomatoes, then sprinkle with oregano. Dress with apple vinegar if desired.

# OVEN-BAKED OMELETTE SALAD

*Eggs are a nutritionally complete food that is living (when fertilized) and extremely easy to digest, provided it is cooked for a short time and at a low temperature. Their proteins are considered superior to meat proteins, because they are easier to assimilate. They also contain vitamins A, E, D, B1, B2 and B12, the latter being extremely important for the nervous system. As regards minerals, it contains plenty of iron, calcium, phosphorus, sulphur and potassium.*

**EASY**

**4 servings**
Cooking time: **20 minutes**
Calories per serving: **140**

1. Preheat the oven to 320° F (160° C).

2. Cut the courgette and potato into small pieces. Remove the hard, woody sections of the herbs and mince them using a mincing knife or blender.

3. Break the eggs into a bowl and add the ricotta cheese, water, chopped parsley, chopped vegetables and chopped herbs. Salt and pepper to taste, then mix well.

4. Pour the contents of the bowl into an oven dish lined with greaseproof paper and cook in the oven for 20 minutes.

5. Clean, wash and delicately dry the salad and arrange a few leaves on a serving dish.

6. When cooked, remove the omelette from the oven, let it cool and cut it into cubes. Place these on the dish, over the salad leaves. Salt and pepper to taste and dress with apple vinegar if desired, then serve.

For the omelette:
4 eggs
1 3/4 oz. (50 g) fresh ricotta cheese
1/2 glass sparkling water
1 tbsp chopped parsley
1 courgette, steamed
1 potato, steamed
1 bunch fresh herbs (rosemary, sage and bay leaf)
Salt
Pepper

For the salad:
2 salad heads (any)
1 tbsp apple vinegar (optional)

# RICE ROULADE

*Venus rice is a highly aromatic and fragrant purple-black whole grain rice. Like all whole grain rice varieties, it is a cereal rich in amino acids and vitamins, making it easy to digest and ideal for slimming diets. It is believed to have detoxifying, refreshing and mildly laxative properties. It was considered very precious in its native China, and indeed in the late 19th century it was grown exclusively for the imperial court, as it was considered an effective aphrodisiac – hence its name.*

EASY

**4 servings**
Preparation time: **20 minutes**
Cooking time: **20 minutes**
Resting time: **20 minutes**
Calories per serving: **120**

2 large leeks
1 3/4 oz. (50 g) Venus rice
1 3/4 oz. (50 g) Basmati rice
2 cups (500 ml) vegetable stock
1 tbsp curry
1 bunch fresh herbs (thyme, oregano and parsley)
Salt
Pepper

*1.* Trim and wash the leeks, then steam them until the leaves are soft and flexible. Allow to cool, then gently remove the leaves.

*2.* Remove the hard, woody sections of the herbs and mince the leaves using a mincing knife or blender.

*3.* Place the Venus rice in a pot with half the herbs, half the stock and double the quantity of rice in water. Cover and allow to boil for 20 minutes. In another pot, cook the Basmati rice with the curry, the other half of the stock and 3/4 cup plus 1 tbsp (200 ml) of water. Once cooked, remove from heat and leave to stand for another 20 minutes.

*4.* Drain the two types of rice and place them in two separate bowls, then salt and pepper to taste.

*5.* Arrange the leek leaves on a chopping board and spoon one type of rice onto their centre (some of the rolls will be filled with Venus rice and others with Basmati rice), leaving free strips of leaf along each edge to be folded inwards, so as to close the "parcels" on all sides. In this way you will prepare rolls of different taste and colour.

*6.* Take four dishes, place a leek leaf folded in half on each plate, and then arrange three rolls on top of one another, the first with one type of filling, the second with another, and the third with the first filling, sprinkling some chopped herbs on each. Garnish the dishes with more chopped herbs and serve at room temperature.

# COURGETTE ROLLS
# WITH SESAME AND CHILLI PEPPER

*Chilli pepper contains antioxidant bioflavonoids, high concentrations of vitamin C, and capsaicin, believed to fight prostate cancer. It also protects the organism against infections and aids digestion and blood circulation.*

**EASY**

**4 servings**
Cooking time: **15-20 minutes**
Calories per serving: **80**

2 courgettes, firm and fairly large
7 oz. (200 g) fish carpaccio (preferably sea bass)
2 tbsp (20 g) white sesame seeds
2 tbsp (20 g) chilli pepper, chopped
Soy sauce
Salt

*1.* Trim and wash the courgettes. Then, using a potato peeler, slice them into long, thin strips.

*2.* Place the fish slices over the courgettes slices and roll half of them with the slice of courgette on the outside and the other half with the slice of fish on the outside. Salt to taste.

*3.* Fasten the rolls by piercing them with a toothpick from side to side.

*4.* Place the sesame seeds and chilli pepper into two separate dishes. Dip the upper side of half the rolls into the sesame and the other half into the chilli pepper. Cook the rolls in an oven dish for around 15-20 minutes or until cooked, then take them out of the oven and let them cool for 5 minutes. Arrange on a dish and serve with soy sauce.

# FENNEL AND FIG SALAD

*Figs are a traditional fruit typical of the Mediterranean. They are packed with energy and especially high in vitamins (A, C, and B complex) and sugars that are easy to digest, associated with minerals such as iron, calcium and phosphorus. They facilitate digestion and are ideal in children's diets. Furthermore, they contain lignin, a vegetable fibre that affects intestinal motility, and are an excellent remedy against constipation.*

EASY

**4 servings**
Preparation time: **10 minutes**
Calories per serving: **115**

1. Clean, wash and slice the fennels thinly, preferably with a slicer or a very sharp knife.

2. Wash 16 figs. If the skin is very tick, gently peel the fruit. If, on the other hand, the figs are very ripe and have a thin skin, then this needn't be discarded as it won't be irritating. Cut the figs into four segments and keep the rest aside for the presentation.

3. Lay the ham out on a chopping board and slice it thinly with a knife.

4. On a serving dish, lay out the sliced fennel, the ham and finally the fig segments. Pepper to taste and serve at room temperature accompanied by the figs kept aside.

**20 black figs, ripe and firm**
**2 fennels**
**3 1/2 oz. (100 g) Parma ham**
**Pepper**

# MACKEREL AND ONION SALAD

*Despite its considerable properties, mackerel is a very cheap oily fish. It is rich in omega-3, B complex vitamins and dietary minerals such as potassium, phosphorus, calcium and sodium. When buying mackerel, ensure it is very fresh, as its delicate meat deteriorates quickly. It can be bought fresh from fish shops when in season, or ready cooked, preserved in brine or oil. It helps fight cholesterol, and is particularly beneficial in low-calorie diets and for one's general wellbeing.*

MEDIUM

**4 servings**
Preparation time: **30 minutes**
Resting time: **30 minutes**
Calories per serving: **170**

1 3/4 lb (800 g) mackerel, fresh
3 lemons
1 orange
1 red onion
1 bunch fresh herbs (hyssop and oregano)
1 small red bell pepper
1 green chilli pepper
1 glass sparkling water
Salt (optional)

*1.* Wash and gut the mackerel. Fill a wide pot with water and bring to the boil. Add the fish and cook for 5 minutes, then drain and leave to cool in a strainer.

*2.* Discard the fish bones, skin and head, and place the fillets in a dish with high edges, big enough to hold the marinade.

*3.* Squeeze a lemon, add the juice to the sparkling water and mix, then pour the liquid on the fish fillets. Leave them to marinade for 30 minutes.

*4.* Clean the vegetables, then peel and slice the onion. Cut a lemon in half, then slice one half and peel and dice the other.

*5.* Cut the red bell pepper and the green chilli pepper into rounds.

*6.* Drain the mackerel from the marinade then dab it dry using kitchen paper and arrange it on a serving dish. Cover it with the onion, pepper, chilli pepper and sliced and diced lemon at will. Squeeze the remaining lemon juice and the orange juice directly onto the plate.

*7.* When serving, sprinkle with the chopped herbs and salt to taste, bearing in mind that mackerel is a flavorsome fish (try it before adding any condiment, because it could be perfect just as it is). The dish is now ready to be served. If you simply can't do without some oil, sprinkle a spoon of extra virgin olive oil onto the dish (remember that a spoon of oil is equivalent to 90 calories).

# SALMON TARTARE

*Salmon contains phosphorus, proteins, iron and calcium. Moreover, it is rich in omega-3 fatty acids, which boosts muscle growth - especially useful for sports people - and lowers cholesterol. Omega-3 is essential in the prevention of blood vessel diseases and to fight visual impairment in the elderly, especially with regard to the macula of the retina.*

**EASY**

**4 servings**
Preparation time: **15 minutes**
Calories per serving: **199**

1 1/3 lbs. (600 g) salmon
2 lemons
4 pressed nori seaweed leaves
1 courgette
Wasabi to taste
Soy sauce to taste
Salt
Pepper

*1.* Squeeze a lemon and keep the juice aside.

*2.* Place the salmon on a chopping board and dice it. Place it in a bowl and add the lemon juice, salt and pepper, then mix.

*3.* Trim and wash the courgette. Then, using a potato peeler, slice it into long, thin strips.

*4.* Slice the remaining lemon. Place some lemon slices on individual dishes and top them with a seaweed leaf and some salmon, trying to give the tartare shape. To this end, you can use a pastry ring: place the nori and the fish inside the ring, and remove it just before serving.

*5.* Decorate the plates with the courgette slices, for example rolling them up and arranging them alongside each portion of tartare. Sprinkle the salmon with freshly ground pepper. Garnish with soy sauce and wasabi at will.

# BRESAOLA CANNOLI

*Bresaola is air-dried, salted beef typical of the Valtellina region of Italy. Its low fat content makes it ideal for use in low-calorie diets. It is high in protein and hence particularly appropriate for sports people. On the other hand, it is not recommended for people who suffer from high blood pressure, due to its high salt content.*

EASY

**4 servings**
Preparation time: **15 minutes**
Calories per serving: **160**

5 1/ 2 oz. (160 g) bresaola
5 oz. (150 g) fresh ricotta
3/4 oz. (20 g) capers in brine
1 tbsp sunflower seeds
2 oranges
1 head of salad
Salt
Pepper

*1.* Wash the oranges and set one aside for the presentation. Peel the rind of the other into little strips, which you will use to garnish the cannoli. If you wish, you can also use the juice of this orange as condiment. Clean, wash and dry the salad and set it aside, wrapped in a damp cloth.

*2.* Chop the capers with the sunflower seeds, keeping one third of the mixture aside as garnish, and add it to the fresh ricotta. Mix the ingredients to form a soft, smooth paste. Salt and pepper to taste, bearing in mind that both the capers and the bresaola are in themselves very flavorsome.

*3.* Lay out each bresaola slice on a smooth surface, such as a marble worktop or a large plate, and spoon the ricotta on top of them. Roll the slices on themselves.

*4.* Place some salad leaves on a plate and arrange the bresaola cannoli on top of them. Garnish with the remaining chopped capers and sunflower seeds. Finally, add the orange peel and, if you wish, the freshly squeezed orange juice.

*5.* Before serving, slice the remaining orange and use the slices to accompany the bresaola cannoli, serving them apart or directly on the dishes.

# RICOTTA, GORGONZOLA AND CELERY SAUCE

*Celery contains potassium, calcium, phosphorus, magnèsium and selenium, as well as a considerable amount of vitamins A, C and K, the latter being essential for blood coagulation processes. It is also a purifying agent, a diuretic and a natural stimulant, due to its aspartic acid content, which is why it was long considered an aphrodisiac.*

**4 servings**
Preparation time: **10 minutes**
Resting time: **30 minutes**
Calories per serving: **100**

*1.* Trim and wash the celery.

*2.* Chop the Gorgonzola cheese into a blender, discarding the rind, and add the ricotta and milk. Blend until smooth.

*3.* Transfer the mixture into four tall, large glasses.

*4.* Arrange some celery sticks into the glasses at will, and the remaining ones on the serving dishes.

*5.* Serve at room temperature or, if it the weather is very hot, place in the refrigerator for 30 minutes before serving accompanied by freshly ground pepper.

**7 oz. (200 g) celery hearts**
**3 1/2 oz. (100 g) ricotta**
**1 3/4 oz. (50 g) Gorgonzola**
**1/2 cup (100 ml) milk**
**Freshly ground pepper**

# SEAFOOD SALAD

*Clams are part of the "Veneridae" family, to which many bivalve molluscs belong, including the famous "carpet shell clams". They are a mine of minerals, such as phosphorus, potassium and calcium, as well as containing considerable amounts of iron, vitamin C, folic acid and retinol. Their high water means they are low in calories, but their distinct flavor makes them a popular ingredient for many delicious Italian recipes.*

MEDIUM

**4 servings**
Preparation time: **40 minutes**
Cooking time: **5 minutes**
Resting time: **30 minutes**
Calories per serving: **250**

1 3/4 lb (800 g) mussels
1 3/4 lb (800 g) clams
7 oz. (200 g) prawn tails
5 oz. (150 g) squid
2 tomatoes
1 bunch basil
Salt
Pepper
Juice of 1 lemon (optional)

1. Wash and slice the tomatoes, then peel and seed them, keeping only the fillets. Drain the excess liquid in a strainer.

2. Soak the mussels and clams separately in water with a spoonful of salt for about 30 minutes, shaking them from time to time, then discard any mussels that have broken or opened. Scrape the shells of the mussels with an iron brush, and remove the beard. Check the clams one by one, tapping them along the slit to ensure they are tightly closed. Discard any that have opened. Rinse the molluscs separately and let them drain.

3. Heat the mussels and clams in two separate pans (they have different opening times), with no condiment. Once opened, remove them from heat and leave to rest until cool, keeping the pans covered. Finally, remove half the molluscs from their shells.

4. Bring a pot full of water to the boil and add the prawn tails, cooking them for 30 seconds, then drain them and rinse them under cold running water to prevent their soft meat from hardening. For a more striking visual impact, do not shell the prawn tails, whereas for a more practical salad, do.

5. Wash the squid and dab them dry with kitchen paper. Cook them in boiling water for 20 seconds, then drain and allow to cool for a few minutes.

6. Clean, wash, dry and mince the basil. Place the mussels, clams, prawn tails, squid and tomatoes in a salad bowl. Add the basil, then salt and pepper to taste. If you like, you can dress the salad with lemon juice. Mix gently, and serve at room temperature.

LIGHT FIRST COURSES ARE A MUST FOR ALL THOSE WHO ARE KEEN TO REMAIN HEALTHY AND FIT, REPLACING CREAMS AND CHEESES WITH HERB AND SPICE BASED FAT-FREE DRESSINGS. THE RESULT? GENUINE FLAVORS, IMPROVED DIGESTION AND A FEW LESS POUNDS!

Light first courses may appear to be an unattainable goal, especially in Italy where oil and butter are used aplenty. Is it possible to prepare a tasty first course without fats? Of course. Will the taste change by adding oil? Naturally. It becomes more appetizing, but also a touch heavier, concealing the other flavors. Fats are found in many foods and are necessary for our health, just like vitamins, trace elements, amino acids and fibres. However, it is important to learn how to choose our fats carefully, using, for example, nuts, sesame seeds or flax seeds, and to avoid sautéing or deep-fat frying, in order to aid our overall wellbeing. We can braise, steam or oven bake, and use herbs and spices to give our preparations that special appetizing touch.

The best allies? Mediterranean herbs, such as rosemary, oregano, sage, parsley, bay leaf and hyssop, and the magnificent chilli pepper, are an absolute must. Or again, if we wish to cross the Italian borders, we can use coriander and a whole host of exotic spices with inviting fragrances. And for those of us who just can't give it up, from time to time we can use a spoon of cold pressed extra virgin olive oil to give an added touch of flavor to our food. When you get used to cooking without oils and animal fats such as butter, lard, beef and goose fat, and so on, flavors will appear cleaner and crisper to the palate, making it easier to detect the various ingredients in the dish. Furthermore, your digestion will improve, and, why not, you might even lose those bothersome extra pounds.

# FIRST COURSES

Fat-free cooking need not revolutionise your kitchen. All it takes are some non-stick pans, some greaseproof paper, a grill, a steamer and an oven, all of which are usually present in our homes. Instead of frying in oil at high temperature, use a ladle of vegetable stock (easily prepared using garlic, onion, celery, carrot, salt and pepper). In this way, your sauces, meats and vegetables will be no less tasty, but much more digestible and lower in calories. Your digestive system will thank you for your choice!

If all this were not enough, then we can use soy cream instead of cow's milk, and ricotta instead of other cheeses, seasoning with freshly ground pepper. And there you have a healthy dish, low in harmful animal fats and rich in useful vegetable fats.

# GAZPACHO

*Cucumber is ideal for low-calorie diets as it contains a considerable amount of tartaric acid, which prevents sugar from transforming into fat. Moreover, it is rich in water, making it a diuretic and purifying agent. It contains minerals such as calcium, potassium and phosphorus, and also vitamins, in particular A, C and those of the B complex. It is a natural kidney cleanser and effectively fights constipation. However, it isn't always easy to digest. In ancient times it was also used as a vermifuge and as a skin treatment, because of its high sulphur content.*

**4 servings**
Preparation time: **15 minutes**
Cooking time: **30 minutes**
Calories per serving: **40**

*1.* Wash, slice, seed and peel the tomatoes, keeping the fillets and draining the excess liquid in a strainer. Clean and chop the chilli pepper, bell pepper, garlic and onion. Trim the cucumber and cut it into rounds.

*2.* Place the vegetables in a blender, keep aside a small amount as garnish and dosing the chilli pepper according to your taste. Season with Tabasco, salt and pepper, then blend to a smooth, creamy paste. Add the ice and blend again.

*3.* Transfer the mixture into a jug, add the remaining chopped vegetables, and serve.

**2 tomatoes**
**1 cucumber**
**1 onion**
**1 clove of garlic**
**1 red bell pepper**
**1 chilli pepper**
**10 ice cubes**
**1 tsp Tabasco sauce**
**Salt**
**Pepper**

# BEAN MINESTRONE

*Beans are the seeds, contained in pods, of the bean plant, belonging to the legume family. They are rich in protein, fibre, potassium, phosphorus, magnesium, and vitamins B2, B3 and B6. Their high fibre content make them an effective laxative, helping to fight constipation and haemorrhoids. These pulses are very nutritious and rich in potassium, phosphorus, calcium, folic acid and retinol, making them particularly suitable in vegetarian and vegan diets.*

**4 servings**
Preparation time: **20 minutes**
Cooking time: **2 hours**
Calories per serving: **161**

1 3/4 lb. (800 g) fresh beans
1 potato
1 courgette
1 onion
2 cloves of garlic
1 bunch fresh herbs (rosemary, sage and thyme)
2 bay leaves
10 chive leaves
1 fresh red chilli pepper
8 slices bread
Salt

1. Wash, peel and dice the potato. Peel and mince the garlic and onion. Trim and dice the courgette. Toast the bread in the oven for about 5 minutes at 400° F (200° C).

2. Place the herbs, bay leaves and chilli pepper in a cheesecloth bag and tie it up with kitchen twine.

3. Shell the beans, wash them and place them into a saucepan. Add the vegetables, about 1 litre of water and the bag of herbs, and cook for about 2 hours or until the beans and vegetables are of the desired consistency.

4. Once cooked, remove the bag of herbs and the chilli pepper. Remove one third of the beans and keep them aside. With an immersion blender, process the mixture until smooth and creamy.

5. Add the remaining beans to the mixture. Stir, season with salt, and add the freshly cut chives.

6. Dish up and garnish with slices of toasted bread. In regions where Parmesan cheese is produced, it is customary to add some rind to the soup, washed and dried, for added flavor (remember that 3 1/2 oz./100 grams) of Parmesan cheese is equivalent to 374 calories).

# CHICKPEA SOUP WITH ROSEMARY

*Chickpeas are the seeds of the plant by the same name, native to Anatolia and used from time immemorial in the Mediterranean. They are the third most popular pulse, after beans and soybeans. They contain many proteins, amino acids and fibres, but just 6% of sugars and fats, making them very suitable for all low-calorie and anti-diabetic diets. They help keep the digestive system regular, and are also rich in potassium, phosphorus, calcium and magnesium, as well as vitamins E, C, K and of the B complex*

**EASY**

**4 servings**
Preparation time: **20 minutes**
Cooking time: **2 hours**
Resting time: **8 hours**
Calories per serving: **323**

8 3/4 oz. (250 g) dried chickpeas
1 onion
1 clove of garlic
1 sprig of rosemary
4 1/4 cup (1 l) vegetable stock
4 slices toasted whole-wheat bread
Salt
Pepper

*1.* Soak the chickpeas in water for 8 hours, then wash them several times and drain them.

*2.* Peel and mince the garlic and onion.

*3.* Discard the hard, woody parts from the rosemary (keeping aside the best as garnish), and chop it finely. Add it to the chopped garlic and onion.

*4.* In a non-stick pan large enough to hold the stock, toast the garlic, onion and rosemary for a few minutes, then season with salt and pepper. When the ingredients start to give off a pleasant odour, add the chickpeas and vegetable stock. Bring to the boil over high heat, then cover and reduce the heat. Cook for about 2 hours, checking regularly to ensure the stock does not overly reduce (if necessary, add a little boiling water).

*5.* Once cooked, add more salt and pepper.

*6.* Serve the chickpea soup in a bowl and garnish with rosemary and toasted bread. The soup is very tasty and does not require any oil. However, if you wish you can pour a spoon of either walnut oil or extra virgin olive oil directly into the soup (remember that a spoonful of oil is equivalent to 90 calories).

# CREAM OF PUMPKIN SOUP WITH SESAME SEEDS

*Pumpkin is a low-calorie food with many nutritional properties. It contains minerals such as calcium, iron, potassium and phosphorus, and is also a source of B-complex vitamins and vitamins A and C. Moreover, it is rich in fibres, that help keep the digestive system regular. It has soothing, digestive and refreshing properties, useful for our general wellbeing and to cleanse the kidneys, as well as being a valuable ally for low-calorie diets.*

**4 servings**
Preparation time: **15 minutes**
Cooking time: **45 minutes**
Calories per serving: **150**

2 1/4 lb. (1 kg) pumpkin
2 leeks
2 shallots
4 1/4 cup (1 l) vegetable stock
3/4 cup (200 g) soy cream
2 tbsp (20 g) light sesame seeds
2 tbsp (20 g) dark sesame seeds
Salt
Pepper

1. Cut the pumpkin into pieces, discarding the seeds, stringy parts and rind. Trim and wash the leeks, then chop them into small pieces. Peel and slice the shallots.

2. Pour the vegetable stock into a pot and cook the pumpkin, leek and shallot until they break up. From time to time, use a fork to check when the vegetables are soft enough to be blended smoothly. Set aside about 30 minutes cooking time on low heat, keeping the pot covered.

3. When cooked, process with an immersion blender directly in the pot, then reduce the mixture until thick and creamy (this should take just a few minutes on high heat). Add the soy cream, salt and pepper. Stir and remove from heat.

4. When serving, transfer the pumpkin soup into four bowls and garnish with sesame seeds at will.

# CREAM OF SPELT SOUP

*Spelt is a cereal that comes in hard brownish or yellowish grains. It has been used in the Mediterranean for as many as 6,000 years. Rich in phosphorus, potassium, magnesium and vitamins A, B2 and B3, it is high in fibres and helps keep the digestive system regular. It is also believed to fight cancer of the gastro-intestinal tract. Moreover, as it gives a sense of fullness and performs a mild laxative effect, it is ideal for slimming diets. However, it is not suitable for coeliacs or for those who suffer from gluten intolerance and irritable bowel syndrome.*

EASY

**4 servings**
Preparation time: **15 minutes**
Cooking time: **40 minutes**
Calories per serving: **380**

7 oz. (200 g) cracked spelt
(Farro Spezzato D.O.P.)
1/2 cup (150 g) soy cream
4 1/4 cup (1 l) vegetable stock
1 courgette
1 onion
1 celery stalk
1 clove of garlic
1 bunch fresh herbs (thyme,
oregano and parsley)
2 tbsp (20 g) light sesame
seeds
2 tbsp (20 g) dark sesame
seeds
1 3/4 oz. (50 g) boiled
chickpeas
12 slices toasted bread
Salt
Pepper

1. In a pot, bring the vegetable stock to the boil.

2. Trim, wash and dice the courgette. Peel and chop the garlic and onion. Wash the celery.

3. Place the herbs in a cheesecloth bag and tie it up with kitchen twine.

4. Boil the vegetables and herbs in the stock for about 30 minutes. Once cooked, remove the bag, blend the vegetables and add the spelt. Cook for another 10 minutes, then remove from heat.

5. Add the soy cream and chickpeas, season with salt and pepper, and stir.

6. When serving, pour a ladle of cream soup into each bowl and garnish with sesame seeds and three slices of toast.

# GREEN SPINACH RAVIOLI

*Spinach is a herbaceous plant whose dark-green leaves are mainly eaten cooked. Native to northern India, it has been known in Europe since the Renaissance. Due to its oxalic acid, spinach can promote the formation of kidney stones and reduce vitamin C reserves. However, it contains vitamin A and folic acid, which promotes the production of red blood cells, as well as a fair amount of minerals, although the idea that they are rich in iron is not quite true. It has laxative, cardiotonic and toning properties.*

**4 servings**
Preparation time: **1 hour**
Cooking time: **2 hours**
Resting time: **20 minutes**
Calories per serving: **350**

**For the ravioli:**
1/4 cup (50 g) durum wheat flour
1 cup (150 g) common wheat flour
2 eggs
1 3/4 oz. (50 g) spinach, boiled and well drained
Salt

**For the filling:**
1 3/4 oz. (50 g) spinach, boiled and well drained
7 oz. (200 g) fresh ricotta
Salt
Pepper

**For the stock:**
10 1/2 oz. (300 g) veal rib rack
1 chicken wing
2 celery stalks
1 carrot
1 onion
1 bunch fresh herbs (rosemary and bay leaf)
Salt
Pepper

1. Place the herbs in a cheesecloth bag and tie it up with kitchen twine. Prepare the carrot, peel the onion and wash the celery, and put them to boil at low heat with the meat and 4 cups (1 litre) of water for about 2 hours, in a covered pot. Add the herbs. Salt and pepper to taste. Once cooked, strain the stock through a strainer and keep it warm until ready to use.

2. To prepare the filling, finely chop the spinach and mix it in a bowl with the ricotta cheese. Salt and pepper to taste and keep the mixture aside until ready to use.

3. Finely blend the spinach for the ravioli dough into a smooth paste to be added to the flours. Pour the flour in a heap onto the wooden rolling board. Make a well in the centre, then crack the eggs into it and add the spinach paste. Beat lightly with a fork, add a pinch of salt and knead with your hands for at least 10 minutes, so that the flour and spinach mix together completely.

4. Let the dough rest for about 20 minutes, wrapped in a kitchen cloth. Using a rolling pin, roll a little dough at a time, keeping the rest covered at all times with the cloth. Flour the rolling board to prevent the dough from sticking. Use a pastry cutter to cut the dough into strips about 12 inches (30 cm) long and 2 inchìes (5 cm) wide. Arrange small heaps of ricotta and spinach filling onto the strips, spacing them by about 1 inch (3 cm). Cover with another strip of dough and press down gently with your fingers to ensure the two strips stick together. Cut the ravioli with the pastry cutter and place them on a floured cloth so that they do not stick to each other.

5. When serving, cook the ravioli in boiling stock and remove them with a skimmer when they reach the desired consistency. Serve the stock in cups and the ravioli on linen napkins.

# DURUM WHEAT CABBAGE RAVIOLI

*Cabbages are typical winter vegetables with edible leaves and flower buds. Very suitable for low-calorie diets, they contain vegetable proteins and vitamin C a-plenty (pound for pound, cabbage has twice the vitamin C content of oranges), as well as vitamins A and K and of the B complex. They are also high in minerals such as copper, iron, calcium and phosphorus. They are used in nutraceutics to treat ulcerative colitis and gastric ulcers, and to facilitate the production of red blood cells and counteract forms of anaemia. They also contain indoles, sulforaphane (a sulphur-based substance, hence its unpleasant smell) and other antioxidants that prevent degenerative diseases.*

**4 servings**
Preparation time: **60 minutes**
Cooking time: **30 minutes**
Resting time: **20 minutes**
Calories per serving: **170**

**For the dough:**
**1/2 cup (100 g) durum wheat flour**
**3/4 cup (100 g) common wheat flour**

**For the filling:**
**7 oz. (200 g) savoy cabbage**
**10 chive leaves**
**3 1/2 oz. (100 g) chicken breast**
**3 1/2 oz. (100 g) fresh ricotta made with cow's milk**
**Pepper**

**For the sauce:**
**Soy sauce**

1. Prepare the savoy cabbage, cutting out the hard core, then wash and cut it into strips. Steam the cabbage and chicken separately, to the desired consistency (approximately 15 minutes).

2. Once cooked, finely chopped the chicken and cabbage, then mince the chives. Pour all the ingredients into a bowl, add the ricotta, and pepper to taste. Stir the mixture and then keep it aside until ready for use.

3. Pour the flours in a heap onto the wooden rolling board. Make a well in the centre, then pour enough water into it (about 1 glass) to produce a smooth mixture. Knead with your hands for at least 10 minutes, until the mixture is smooth and without lumps.

4. Let the dough rest for about 20 minutes, wrapped in a kitchen cloth. Flour a rolling board to prevent the dough from sticking, then, using a rolling pin, roll a little dough at a time to approximately 1 mm thickness, keeping the rest covered at all times with the cloth.

5. With a pastry cutter, cut the dough into 3 inch (8 cm) squares. Place some filling in the centre of the squares, fold them to form a triangle and, with your fingers, ensure the edges stick together, then join two extremities (as if you were making cappelletti). Repeat until all the ingredients are used up, then place the ravioli thus obtained on a floured cloth so that they do not stick to each another.

6. Steam the ravioli for about 5-7 minutes, remove them from the steamer, and serve hot with soy sauce.

# SEAFOOD PENNE

*Mussels are among the most popular shellfish in Italy. They can be eaten raw, dressed with oil and lemon, or au gratin with garlic and parsley, or even served on pasta. They are a light food, very low in fat content, and are therefore suitable for low-calorie diets. They contain antioxidants, proteins, group C and B vitamins, potassium, phosphorus, zinc and iron.*

MEDIUM

**4 servings**
Preparation time: **40 minutes**
Cooking time: **20 minutes**
Resting time: **30 minutes**
Calories per serving: **427**

12 1/2 oz. (350 g) rice penne
1 3/4 lb (800 g) carpet shell clams
2 1/4 lb. (1 kg) mussels
4 ripe tomatoes
1 bunch basil, cleaned
1 tbsp fresh herbs, chopped (oregano and parsley)
1 clove of garlic
Salt
Pepper

1. Wash, slice, seed and peel the tomatoes, keeping the fillets and draining the excess liquid in a strainer. Chop the tomato fillets.

2. Soak the mussels and clams separately in salted water. Let them drain for 30 minutes, shaking from time to time, then discard any mussels that have broken or opened. Scrape the mussel shells with an iron brush, and remove the beard.

3. Check the clams one by one, tapping them along the slit to ensure they are tightly closed. Discard any that have opened.

4. Rinse the molluscs separately and let them drain. Heat the mussels and clams in two different pans (they have different opening times) with no condiment. Once opened, remove them from heat and leave to rest, keeping the pans covered.

5. Remove half the shellfish from their shells and filter the cooking liquid. Preheat the oven to 425° F (220° C).

6. Place the clove of garlic and tomatoes in a large pot (big enough to hold the pasta and the sauce) and cook for 2 minutes on high heat, then add the shellfish and the chopped herbs. Stir, season with salt and pepper, then remove from heat and cover.

7. Boil the penne in plenty of salted water, cook them until they are firm to the bite, and transfer them into the sauce. Mix and pour the pasta into an oven dish, drizzle over a few spoons of the shellfish liquid, and bake for 10 minutes. When cooked, remove the dish from the oven, sprinkle the penne with basil, and serve hot.

# BAKED TAGLIATELLE

*Egg pasta contains starch, which in effect is a difficult to digest sugar. Egg, however, helps to enrich such pasta with a considerable concentration of proteins, making it more nutritiounally valuable than all the other common wheat pastas. As it is high in calories, it should be eaten in moderation, although the lecithin contained in egg yolks helps to reduce the levels of cholesterol in the blood.*

EASY

**4 servings**
Preparation time: **10 minutes**
Cooking time: **20 minutes**
Calories per serving: **368**

**14 oz. (400 g) egg tagliatelle**
**7 oz. (200 g) fresh salmon**
**2 courgettes**
**1/4 oz. (10 g) dried chilli pepper**
**1 bunch fresh sage, chopped**
**Salt**

*1.* Preheat the oven to 425° F (220° C).

*2.* Bone and skin the salmon, then wash, dry and dice it.

*3.* Trim and wash the courgettes, then cut them into rounds. In a non-stick pan, stew the courgettes and half the salmon for about 5 minutes, then flavor with freshly chopped sage.

*4.* Bring to the boil a pot filled with plenty of salted water. Cook the tagliatelle until they are firm to the bite. Transfer the pasta into the pan with the courgettes and salmon, mix well, and season with salt and chilli pepper. Pour the pasta onto sheets of greaseproof paper (one parcel per person), add the remaining salmon and some more sage, then close the parcels and oven bake for 10 minutes.

*5.* When cooked, arrange the parcels in soup plates or deeper bowls, and serve with chilli pepper and sage. The salmon will make the pasta nicely moist and seasoned, but if you wish you can add a spoonful of oil directly into the dish (remember that a spoonful of oil is equivalent to 90 calories).

# WHOLE-WHEAT GEMELLI PASTA WITH PEANUTS

*Peanuts are legumes composed of 30% protein and 40% fat, almost entirely unsaturated, and therefore suitable for fighting vascular diseases. Moreover, they contain antioxidants such as resveratrol and oleic acid (believed to have anti-cancer properties, especially of the colon), as well as fibres, vitamin E and many minerals such as potassium, phosphorus, manganese, magnesium, zinc and copper.*

**4 servings**
Preparation time: **10 minutes**
Cooking time: **10 minutes**
Calories per serving: **420**

12 1/2 oz. (350 g)
whole-wheat gemelli pasta
1 oz. (30 g) peanuts
2 carrots, fresh
3 1/2 oz. (100 g) oatmeal cream
5 sprigs of fresh hyssop
Salt
Pepper

*1.* Shell the peanuts and grind them coarsely in a mortar. In a bowl, add them to the oatmeal cream, stir well, and keep aside until ready for use. Clean and wash the hyssop, then wrap it in kitchen paper until ready for use.

*2.* Peel, wash and dry the carrots, then cut them into thin strips with the aid of a potato peeler.

*3.* Bring to the boil a pot filled with plenty of salted water and cook the pasta for the time indicated on the package.

*4.* Drain the pasta and stir it into the oatmeal cream and peanuts, then add the carrots. Season with pepper to taste.

*5.* Serve the pasta hot, flavoring and decorating it with hyssop leaves.

# CRISPY LINGUINE WITH ALMONDS

*Almonds can be used as nuts, and also for the preparation of first courses, second courses and desserts. Rich in unsaturated fatty acids, vegetable proteins and sugars, they help keep cholesterol low and the digestive system regular. They contain many important minerals such as potassium, phosphorus, calcium and zinc, as well as a high percentage of dietary fibres, B and E group vitamins, and folic acid. However, they are particularly high in calories: 542 calories per 100 grams!*

EASY

**4 servings**
Preparation time: **20 minutes**
Cooking time: **10 minutes**
Calories per serving: **378**

12 1/2 oz. (350 g) durum
wheat linguine
1 oz. (30 g) almonds
3/4 oz. (20 g) wild fennel
50 ml Passito wine from
Pantelleria
1/2 cup (100 ml) vegetable
stock
Salt
Pepper

*1.* Grind the almonds in a mortar or blender, keeping some aside as garnish. Clean and gently chop the wild fennel (leaving some tufts aside), then heat the vegetable stock.

*2.* Pour the Passito wine from Pantelleria into a large non-stick pan, let the alcohol evaporate on high heat, then add the ground almonds, wild fennel, salt and pepper. Spray regularly with spoonfuls of vegetable stock, and stir to obtain a smooth cream (this should take just a few minutes).

*3.* Bring to the boil a pot filled with plenty of salted water, and cook the pasta for the time indicated on the package. Drain and transfer the paste onto the sauce, then stir. Place the pan on high heat and let the liquids evaporate, lightly toasting the linguine. Season with salt and pepper to taste.

*4.* Serve hot, garnished with almonds and tufts of wild fennel.

# SPELT LASAGNE
# WITH WALNUTS AND CATALOGNA CHICORY

*Catalogna chicory has been used in Europe since the most remote antiquity. Rich in minerals such as calcium, potassium and phosphorus, it also contains vitamins A and C. It is low in calories and very suitable for slimming diets, because it reduces the absorption of sugars into the intestine by incorporating them into its fibres, which are subsequently eliminated. With its vasodilatory properties, it also stimulates the entire cardiovascular system.*

MEDIUM

**4 servings**
Preparation time: **30 minutes**
Cooking time: **20 minutes**
Calories per serving: **450**

10 1/2 oz. (300 g) spelt lasagne
1 1/3 lbs. (600 g) Catalogna chicory
1 3/4 oz. (50 g) walnuts, shelled
3/4 cup (200 g) soy bechamel
1/2 cup (50 g) breadcrumbs
Salt

1. Coarsely grind the walnuts in a mortar. Add the breadcrumbs and toast in a non-stick pan for a few minutes. Shake the pan constantly so that the mixture does not burn.

2. Preheat the oven to 425° F (220° C).

3. Clean, wash and chop the chicory, then let it boil until soft, checking its consistency from time to time with a fork. When cooked, pour the vegetables into a strainer and let them drain for a few minutes.

4. Bring to the boil a pot filled with plenty of salted water and dip the lasagne into it a few sheets at a time. When soft, remove them with a skimmer and lay them out on a cotton or linen cloth.

5. Line a baking dish with a layer of lasagne and season them with the chicory, bechamel, walnuts and breadcrumbs. Cover with another layer of pasta and repeat until the all the ingredients are used up, keeping some walnuts and breadcrumbs aside for the garnish.

6. Brown in the oven for about 10 minutes and serve, sprinkled with ground walnuts and breadcrumbs.

# VEGETABLE ROLLS

*Egg is rich in fat and protein, but also in lecithin, widely appreciated for its health benefits, and in particular its ability to increase "good cholesterol" and reduce "bad cholesterol" levels in the blood. Many of the fats it contains are unsaturated and therefore useful for the cardiovascular system. However, sufferers of gallstones and liver diseases should limit its intake. The steamed vegetables with which these rolls are filled are rich in fibre, have laxative properties and help reduce fat absorption.*

MEDIUM

**4 servings**
Preparation time: **25 minutes**
Cooking time: **30 minutes**
Calories per serving: **250**

**For the roll:**
2 cups (500 ml) milk
2 eggs
1 1/4 cup (200 g) wheat meal

**For the filling:**
1 courgette
1 aubergine
1 tomato
1 yellow bell pepper
1 red bell pepper
7 oz. (200 g) soy bechamel
1/2 cup (100 ml) vegetable stock
Nutmeg to taste
Salt
Pepper

*1.* Heat the vegetable stock and keep warm until ready to use.

*2.* Trim, wash and chop the aubergine, tomato and peppers into small pieces. Trim, wash and dice the courgette.

*3.* Stew the vegetables in a non-stick pan for about 5 minutes (or longer, if you like them very soft), basting them, when necessary, with some vegetable stock. Once they have reached the desired consistency, pour the vegetables into a bowl and add the bechamel. Salt and pepper to taste, season with nutmeg, cover, and let stand until ready to use.

*4.* Break the eggs into a bowl, then pour in the milk and flour, stirring with an electric mixer until the mixture is smooth and free of lumps.

*5.* Grease a 8 inch (20 cm) non-stick pan with kitchen paper soaked in oil, then ladle in a thin layer of mixture, covering the bottom of the pan. Leave to cook for about a minute. Once cooked, the pancake will come away easily from the pan: turn it over and allow it to cook on the other side. Repeat until all the mixture is used up.

*6.* Remove from heat and place the pancakes thus obtained on a plate. Fill them with stewed vegetables, then roll them up, and, using a sharp knife, gently cut them into two or more pieces, depending on the size required. Arrange them on a baking dish.

*7.* Before serving, heat the pancakes in the oven at 400° F (200° C) for about 10 minutes.

# STUFFED PANCAKES

*The nutritional and dietary benefits of eggs, combined with their ease of digestion, make them a very important food for athletes. They are in absolute terms the most nutritious and energetic food available to us. They contain complete proteins, generally associated with fatty and high-calorie substances, but are also rich in vitamins and minerals. Egg yolks contain lecithins and triglycerides in low concentrations, due to the presence of monounsaturated fats that are beneficial for the organism.*

EASY

**4 servings**
Preparation time: **20 minutes**
Cooking time: **20 minutes**
Calories per serving: **277**

**For the pancakes:**
**2 cups (500 ml) milk**
**2 eggs**
**1 1/4 cup (200 g) wheat meal**
**1 bunch chive leaves**

**For the filling:**
**4 tomatoes**
**1 bell pepper**
**1 onion**
**1/2 cup (100 ml) vegetable stock, hot**
**Salt**
**Pepper**

1. Wash, peel and cut the tomatoes, and drain the excess liquid in a strainer. Cut the pepper, remove the stem, seeds and white parts, then cut it into small pieces. Peel and slice the onion. Stew the vegetables in a non-stick pan for about 10 minutes, basting them as necessary with spoonfuls of stock, and salt and pepper to taste. When ready, remove them from heat and let stand, keeping the pan covered.

2. Break the eggs into a bowl, then pour in the milk and flour, stirring with an electric mixer until the mixture is smooth and free of lumps.

3. Grease a 10 inch (25 cm) non-stick pan with kitchen paper soaked in oil, then ladle in a thin layer of mixture, covering the bottom of the pan. Leave to cook for about a minute. Once cooked, the pancake will come away easily from the pan: turn it over and allow it to cook on the other side. Repeat until all the mixture is used up.

4. Remove from heat and place the pancakes thus obtained on a plate. Place a spoonful of vegetable filling on each pancake and close them up like a parcel, tying them up gently with chive leaves.

5. Before serving, heat the pancakes in the oven at 425° F (220° C) for about 10 minutes. Serve the pancakes with any left over filling.

# MILLET SALAD

*Millet, a member of the grass family, is a highly digestible cereal high in vitamins E and of the B complex. It contains various minerals, in particular potassium, phosphorus, magnesium, calcium, manganese, iron, zinc and selenium, and amino acids, such as glutamic acid, aspartic acid, alanine, arginine, cystine, serine, valine, tryptophan, proline and isoleucine. As a result, it boasts effective toning and energising properties, and is suitable for coeliacs. It also contains a considerable concentration of natural acetylsalicylic acid, and is therefore believed to strengthen hair and to act as a mild anti-inflammatory.*

 EASY

**4 servings**
Preparation time: **10 minutes**
Cooking time: **15 minutes**
Resting time: **20 minutes**
Calories per serving: **271**

*1.* Clean, wash and cut the tomatoes, carrot and pepper into small pieces. Trim, wash and cut the courgette into rounds. Peel and thinly slice the onion. Put all the vegetables in a bowl, then salt and pepper to taste.

*2.* Pour the millet into a pot with twice the quantity of water, cover, and allow to boil on low heat for 15 minutes. Remove from heat and let stand for about 20 minutes.

*3.* Drain the millet of any unabsorbed liquid and add it to the vegetables, mixing well.

*4.* Place the salad in a serving dish or individual bowls and serve at room temperature.

**1 cup (200 g) millet**
**3 tomatoes**
**1 courgette**
**1 carrot**
**1 red bell pepper**
**1 red onion**
**Salt**
**Pepper**

# RYE SALAD WITH TOFU

*Rye, grown in Europe for thousands of years, withstands harsh weather conditions. Most "black" breads are made with this cereal's flour. Rye contains lysine, an amino acid rarely present in other cereals, and is high in fibre, as well as in minerals, vitamin E and B-complex vitamins. It is believed to effectively prevent constipation and bowel cancer. It also boasts considerable energising and anti-sclerotic properties.*

EASY

**4 servings**
Preparation time: **10 minutes**
Cooking time: **30 minutes**
Resting time: **2 hours and 20 minutes**
Calories per serving: **250**

7 oz. (200 g) rye
8 celery stalks
1 red bell pepper, small
1 carrot
7 oz. (200 g) tofu
1 lemon
Salt
Pepper

1. Clean, wash and chop the carrot and pepper into small pieces. Wash and dry the celery, removing the hard parts and setting aside the best leaves for the garnish, then cut it into thin rounds. Put the vegetables in a bowl, then salt and pepper to taste.

2. Drain the tofu and cut it into pieces. Add it to the vegetables.

3. Rinse the rye grains in a strainer under cold running water, then transfer them into a bowl and leave to soak for 2 hours.

4. Pour the rye into a pot with twice the quantity of water, cover, and allow to boil on low heat for 30 minutes. Remove from heat and let stand for about 20 minutes.

5. Drain the rye grains of any excess liquid, then add them to the vegetables and stir. Salt and pepper to taste, then season with freshly squeezed lemon juice and garnish with fresh celery leaves.

6. Serve the salad at room temperature. It can be stored in the refrigerator for a few days.

# SPELT SALAD

*Carrots, available all year round, are high in beta-carotene (which the body converts into vitamin A), as well as C, E and B group vitamins. They are also rich in minerals such as phosphorous, calcium, potassium, sodium, magnesium and copper. The presence of sugars, dextrose and levulose means it should not be consumed in great quantities by diabetics.*

**EASY**

**4 servings**
Preparation time: **10 minutes**
Cooking time: **20 minutes**
Resting time: **35 minutes**
Calories per serving: **273**

**7 oz. (200 g) spelt**
**14 oz. (400 g) cherry tomatoes**
**1 carrot**
**1 courgette**
**1 oz. (30 g) raisins**
**Salt**
**Pepper**

**To garnish:**
**4 courgette flowers**

*1.* Wash and cut the tomatoes in half. Clean, wash and peel the carrot and chop it into small pieces. Trim, wash and cut the courgette, first in half and then into rounds. Place the vegetables in a bowl.

*2.* Soak the raisins in a bowl of warm water for 10 minutes, then squeeze them to remove the liquid.

*3.* Wash the spelt and leave it to soak for 30 minutes, then drain. Pour it into a pot with twice the quantity of water, cover, and allow to cook on low heat for 20 minutes. Remove from heat and let stand for about 5 minutes. Drain the cereal and rinse under cold running water to stop it cooking. Transfer it into the bowl with the vegetables. Salt and pepper to taste, then add the raisins.

*4.* Pour the spelt into individual bowls and garnish each plate with a courgette flower.

# BAKED SEAWEED
# WITH VEGETABLES AND BASMATI RICE

*Mange tout are green or pale yellow pods that are soft and crisp in texture. Completely edible, they are 70% made up of water, and contain a high percentage of potassium, phosphorus and calcium. They also contain a high concentration of vitamin C, folic acid and retinol.*

**4 servings**
Preparation time: **10 minutes**
Cooking time: **20 minutes**
Calories per serving: **180**

4 sheets nori seaweed
7 oz. (200 g) mange tout
3 1/2 oz. (100 g) Basmati rice, steamed
12 mussels
8 clams
1 tsp. fresh parsley, chopped
1 clove of garlic
1 tsp (0.5 g) saffron
1 bunch chives or raffia
Salt
Pepper

1. Wash the mange tout, then steam them until they reach the desired consistency.

2. Heat the seafood in a pan with no seasoning. Once opened, remove them from heat and take them out of their shells. Strain the cooking liquid and use two spoonfuls to dissolve the saffron.

3. Place the rice, seafood, freshly chopped mange tout and saffron stock in a bowl, stirring well. Season with salt and pepper.

4. Peel and mince the garlic and add it, with the parsley, to the bowl with the other ingredients. Stir, then make little cones with the sheets of nori seaweed and fill them with rice.

5. Tie the cones with chive leaves or raffia, and serve at room temperature. If desired, accompany them with soy sauce.

# CURRY RICE
# WITH VEGETABLES AND PRAWNS

*Curry is a blend of various spices, including chilli pepper, coriander, cumin, cinnamon, ginger and cardamom. The mixture aids digestion, helps fight nausea, and disinfects the digestive system. Its tantalising scent stimulates the appetite and the metabolism.*

MEDIUM

**4 servings**
Preparation time: **20 minutes**
Cooking time: **20 minutes**
Calories per serving: **300**

7 oz. (200 g) Basmati rice
20 asparagus
8 prawn tails
1 shallot
1 red bell pepper, small
1 courgette, small
1 aubergine, small
1 tbsp curry
2 cups (500 ml) vegetable stock
4 green chilli peppers
Salt
Pepper

*1.* Clean the vegetables and chop them up separately, setting aside half of the asparagus whole. Heat the shallot in a pan over medium heat with a tablespoon of stock. When it begins to dry up, add the vegetables and spoon over the rest of the stock. Cook for 5 minutes and season with curry.

*2.* Remove the prawn shells and add them to the vegetables. Cook for 2 minutes, stirring continuously, then remove from heat and set aside until ready to use.

*3.* Boil the rice in salted water and drain when it has reached the desired consistency. Add half the vegetables and stir. Season with salt and pepper.

*4.* Steam the remaining asparagus for a few minutes, then allow to cool at room temperature.

*5.* When serving, use a round 3 inch (8 cm) pastry ring to create individual rice portions. Pour the remaining vegetables on top and serve with the steamed asparagus and a green chilli pepper.

# OYSTER CHOWDER

*Oysters are a mollusc rich in proteins and minerals such as zinc, iron, phosphorus, selenium and calcium. They are traditionally known for their supposed aphrodisiac properties. This is perhaps due to their high zinc content which, favouring the production of hormones such as testosterone, improves sexual potency and male fertility. These molluscs also contain polyunsaturated fatty acids, excellent for the prevention of vascular diseases.*

MEDIUM

**4 servings**
Preparation time: **20 minutes**
Cooking time: **1 hour**
Calories per serving: **120**

**For the stock:**
4 prawns
2 scampi
2 clams, washed and drained
5 mussels, washed and drained
1 shallot
1 glass white wine
10 basil leaves
10 parsley leaves

**For the soup:**
4 oysters per person
10 basil leaves
Salt

1. To prepare the stock, gently clean, wash and dry the parsley and basil, and chop them finely. Put 1 litre of water in a pot and boil the seafood (except the oysters) and the peeled and sliced shallot for half an hour on low heat. Add the chopped herbs and wine.

2. During cooking, remove the shells of the mussels and clams.

3. Once cooked, squeeze the stock's ingredients with a fork to release their juices. Strain, then keep the stock warm until ready to use.

4. To prepare the soup, first steep the oysters in salted water for about half an hour, then scrape them one by one and clean them thoroughly.

5. Stew the oysters in a non-stick pan until they open. Remove from heat and, using a pair of gloves to avoid burns, remove one of the two valves.

6. Place a ladle of stock in individual bowls, and serve with four oysters each.

LOW-CALORIE DIETS OFTEN REVOLVE AROUND MEATS, EITHER STEAMED OR GRILLED. LIGHTLY SEASONED FISH, TOFU, RICOTTA AND EGGS CAN ALSO BE USED, FOR A TRULY HEALTHY DIET. ALWAYS GIVE PRECEDENCE TO EXTRA VIRGIN OLIVE OIL, AND ONLY ADD IT ONCE YOUR DISH IS COOKED.

Main courses are a fascinating world of white and red meats, fish, eggs and cheeses. They are often the most important dish of the meal. The latest dietary recommendations advise against associating animal protein with excessive fat, and – contrary to popular belief – against using them in demanding meals, consisting of many courses.

Latest research indicates that animal proteins should be consumed no more than three or four times a week, fish two or three times, and eggs and cheese twice, with the remaining meals revolving around other foods such as vegetables, fruits and pulses. However, our fast-paced lifestyle often means we have to snatch the time for our meals, simply opening the fridge and gobbling whatever we can in 5 minutes flat. Dietary research specialists recommend setting aside an appropriate amount of time for our meals, scheduling our food intake and choosing our ingredients with care. Thus, we should prefer certain cooking techniques over others, carefully assess the calorie content of our food, and remember that limiting fat intake not only aids digestion, but also reduces the tendency to accumulate fat.

What meats can help us reduce our calorie intake? There's white chicken and turkey meats, the fat of which is mainly found in the skin, that can easily be removed; pork, which similarly accumulates fat cells in specific parts of the body, such as under the rind; and fish, which, while lipid-rich, favours our well-being through their omega-3 fatty acids. Eggs are a chapter onto themselves. Their particularly interesting properties make them a real treasure trove for

# MAIN COURSES

vegetarians. Cheeses – especially seasoned ones, which are easier to digest – are a welcome addition to the diet, although only in moderation. But it is the choice of cooking technique that is really important when preparing light, low-calorie meals. A baked omelette is certainly no less appetizing than a fried one. In fact, in addition to being extremely tasty, soft in texture and easy to digest, the enveloping warmth of the oven helps preserve the delicate flavor and fragrance of fresh eggs. Meatballs can also become crunchy delights when baked, and delicious treats when stewed in tomato sauce. Moreover, almost all protein foods lose their liquid and fat when grilled, making the fibres soft and tasty (tuna, for example, is at its best grilled). Steaming should not be overlooked for fish and seafood, and nor should baking in a salt crust, which preserves the food's nutrients.

# VEGETABLE QUICHE

*Bell peppers are primarily made up of water (more than 90% of their weight), as well as 1-2% vegetable protein and 2-3% sugars. Fats make up just 0.2-0.4% of the total. They are a good source of fibres, and also include pectin and different types of cellulose. Their vitamin A and C content is high (the latter found in greater quantities than in cabbage and spinach), and both these vitamins are useful antioxidants for the prevention of degenerative diseases. Finally, peppers are also a source of iron, copper and manganese.*

EASY

**4 servings**
Preparation time: **15 minutes**
Cooking time: **20 minutes**
Resting time: **5 minutes**
Calories per portion: **250**

*1.* Preheat the oven to 400° F (200° C). Peel and cut the Trevisana chicory into small pieces. Wash the pepper, remove the stem, and cut it along the grooves. Remove the seeds and white part, then chop it into small squares.

*2.* Beat the egg, ricotta and cream with a whisk, seasoning with salt, pepper and nutmeg to taste, until the mixture is smooth and free of lumps.

*3.* Place the pizza dough on greaseproof paper and roll it out wafer thin with a rolling pin (about 2 mm). Transfer the paper and dough into a baking sheet.

*4.* Pour the egg-based filling onto the dough and distribute the pepper and chicory over it at will. Bake for about 20 minutes, then remove from the oven and let the quiche cool for 5 minutes. Cut into portions and serve.

**7 oz. (200 g) ready pizza dough**
**1 yellow bell pepper**
**1 heads Trevisana chicory**
**1/2 cup (100 g) soy cream**
**1 3/4 oz. (50 g) ricotta**
**1 egg**
**Nutmeg to taste**
**Salt**
**Pepper**

# CHICKEN AND TOFU MEATBALLS

*Tofu is a soy cheese originating in China. Its Chinese name is* doufu, *but in Western recipes and menus it is more often found in its Japanese version, as it is very popular throughout the East, and in particular in the Land of the Rising Sun. Its high vegetable protein and essential amino acid content makes it suitable for vegan and vegetarian diets. Moreover, being low in calories, it can be used in all types of diet. It also contains minerals such as calcium, potassium, iron and phosphorus, as well as substances such as lecithins, capable of reducing blood cholesterol levels and systolic blood pressure.*

MEDIUM

**4 servings**
Preparation time: **35 minutes**
Cooking time: **10 minutes**
Calories per portion: **105**

**For the meatballs:**
3 1/2 oz. (100 g) chicken breast
3 1/2 oz. (100 g) tofu
1 aubergine
2 cups (500 ml) vegetable stock
5 chive leaves
5 sprigs parsley
White flour as needed
Salt
Pepper

**For the sauce:**
1 tbsp chopped herbs (parsley, oregano and chives)
14 oz. (400 g) peeled tomatoes
1 onion
1 clove of garlic
Salt

1. To prepare the sauce, peel the garlic and the onion and chop them finely, then put them into a non-stick pan (big enough to contain the meatballs) with the tomatoes and herbs. Salt to taste. Cook for about 15 minutes, until the liquid reduces at least by half. Turn off the heat, cover the pan and set it aside until ready to use.

2. Steam the chicken for about 15 minutes. Once cooked, chop it finely and place it in a bowl. Drain the tofu and cut it into pieces, then transfer it into the bowl with the meat.

3. Clean, wash and halve the aubergine. Cut one half into slices and toast them lightly in a non-stick pan with no condiment. These will be used as garnish. Peel the skin off the other half and chop the pulp, then put it in the bowl with the chicken.

4. Mince the chives and parsley, add them to the other ingredients, season with salt and pepper, and mix well until the mixture is smooth.

5. Prepare the meatballs by taking a small amount of mixture at a time and rolling it into a ball with your hands. Continue until all the mixture is used up. Flour a work surface and roll the meatballs so as to flour them well.

6. Gently transfer the meatballs into the pan with the sauce and cook them over low heat for about 10 minutes. If necessary, spray them with vegetable stock.

7. When cooked, place a slice of aubergine on each plate and arrange some meatballs on top. Serve hot.

# SPICY CHICKEN WITH RICE

*White meat boasts highly digestible proteins. It is excellent in fighting fatigue, increasing antibodies and renewing tissues. Chicken breast, in particular, contains 75% water, while proteins make up 23% of the total, and fat less than 1%. It also contains vitamins A, C and E, and those of the B complex, as well as minerals such as magnesium, zinc, copper, selenium, potassium and iron. Chicken, therefore, is very suitable to keep calories down in low-fat diets, while being a good source of energy.*

EASY

**4 servings**
Preparation time: **15 minutes**
Cooking time: **20 minutes**
Calories per portion: **292**

**7 oz. (200 g) rice**
**14 oz. (400 g) chicken breast**
**1 tsp curry**
**1 tsp paprika**
**2 tbsp tomato paste**
**1 onion**
**1 clove of garlic**
**2 cups (500 ml) vegetable stock**
**1 sprig fresh rosemary**
**Salt**

1. Peel and mince the garlic and onion. Clean, wash and dry the rosemary.

2. Pour the rice into a non-stick pan and season it with the chopped garlic and onion on high heat. After about a minute, add the tomato paste and stock. Stir and cook over low heat for about 15 minutes. While it is cooking, add salt to taste, then remove from heat and set aside covered until ready for use.

3. Cut the chicken breast into thin slices. Place the curry and paprika on a chopping board, then roll the chicken in the spices, pressing lightly with your hands.

4. Cook the chicken in a non-stick pan over high heat for 3-4 minutes, turning often and adding salt to taste.

5. When cooked, arrange the chicken on top of the rice, either in a dish or bowl. Season and garnish the dish with some rosemary. Serve hot or at room temperature.

# DUCK FILLET WITH GRAPEFRUIT

*Grapefruit is a low-calorie fruit largely made of water. It contains pectin and vitamins A, C and E, as well as bitter substances that strengthen the stomach and lungs. It exerts a purifying action on liver and kidneys. Furthermore, its antioxidants effectively fight degenerative diseases. Its juice may increase the anxiolytic effects of psychotropic drugs.*

MEDIUM

**4 servings**
Preparation time: **15 minutes**
Cooking time: **15-20 minutes**
Calories per portion: **300**

**1 duck breast,
whole (about 1 3/4 lb./800 g)
2 grapefruits
Salt
Pepper**

1. Wash the grapefruits and peel one of them using a potato peeler or a sharp knife: be careful to leave the pith on the fruit (which is very bitter) and, if necessary, scrape it off the peel. Cut the peel into matchsticks and set them aside until ready for use.

2. Wash the duck breast and, if it is still whole, cut it in half to obtain two fillets, removing any feathers. Dry the duck well and make little slits in the skin to ensure the fillets do not curl during cooking.

3. Squeeze and strain the juice of the second grapefruit, and cut the first into segments as garnish for the fillet.

4. Heat a non-stick pan over high heat, place the two fillets skin side down, and let them brown. After about 4-5 minutes, turn them over and add some grapefruit juice and the chopped peel. Salt and pepper to taste, then cover.

5. Cook the fillets for about 15 minutes on high heat, turning regularly every 2-3 minutes and spraying when needed with spoonfuls of grapefruit juice.

6. When serving, remove the peel, and with a very sharp knife, cut the duck into thin slices. Arrange these on serving dishes, and garnish with the grapefruit segments and matchsticks at will.

# TURKEY KEBABS
# MARINATED IN SOY SAUCE

*Soy sauce, known in Japan as* shoyu, *is a fermented sauce that originated in China, where it is called* jiangyou. *Buddhist monks used it to give food a meat flavor, as their religion required them to adopt a vegetarian diet. Its most worthy nutritional property is its high content of antioxidants - 10 times higher than that of red wine - and its effective antidegenerative and digestive action. However, its salt content makes it unsuitable for those suffering from hypertension and in low-sodium diets.*

**EASY**

**4 servings**
Preparation time: **15 minutes**
Cooking time: **10 minutes**
Marinading time: **20 minutes**
Calories per portion: **150**

**14 oz. (400 g) turkey breast**
**1 yellow bell pepper**
**1 red bell pepper**
**1 courgette**
**1/2 cup (100 ml) soy sauce**
**1 tbsp mixed spices (coriander, cardamom, turmeric, curry, chilli pepper and pepper)**
**Salt flavored with turmeric (optional)**

*1.* Cut the meat into pieces big enough to be skewered.

*2.* Pour the soy sauce into a bowl. In a mortar, coarsely chop the spices, then pour them into the sauce. This can be seasoned to taste with turmeric-flavored or plain salt, but bear in mind that soy sauce is in itself very salty, and so it is advisable to add the salt at the last minute, when you are ready to cook the meat.

*3.* Marinade the meat in the flavored soy sauce for about 20 minutes.

*4.* Clean and wash the peppers. Cut them into strips, and then cut these into two or three, depending on the size of the vegetable. Trim, wash and cut the courgette into roughly 1 inch (2-3 cm) rounds.

*5.* Once marinaded, skewer the meat onto wooden sticks, alternating them with the vegetables. Repeat until all the ingredients are used up.

*6.* Heat the griddle or a non-stick pan. When it is ready, cook the kebabs as desired (this will take about 10 minutes), turning them often and spraying them with the marinade (to which you can now add the salt, after tasting) whenever necessary. Serve the kebabs hot.

# CRUSTED PORK FILLET WITH STRAWBERRY JUICE

*Strawberries contain little sugar, and in particular fructose. Therefore, in their natural state they are well tolerated by diabetics. They contain many minerals, such as iron, sodium, potassium, calcium, phosphorus and magnesium. These fruits are also rich in vitamins, in particular vitamin C, and in antioxidants such as salicylic and ellagic acid, which are believed to fight the formation of cancer cells.*

**4 servings**
Preparation time: **10 minutes**
Cooking time: **20 minutes**
Calories per portion: **210**

1 1/3 lbs. (600 g) pork fillet
14 oz. (400 g) strawberries
1 bunch thyme
1 sprig of rosemary
4 bay leaves
1 bunch sage
3/4 cup plus 1 tbsp (200 ml) dry white wine
Salt
Pepper

*1.* Remove all the hard, woody parts from the herbs. Set aside the best leaves as garnish. Finely chop the rest using a mincing knife or blender, then sprinkle them over a chopping board.

*2.* Roll the fillet onto the bed of herbs, pressing with your hands.

*3.* Wash and chop the strawberries. Purée them in a blender until smooth, keeping some aside, whole, as garnish.

*4.* In a saucepan, brown the meat on all sides for about 20 minutes over high heat. Given that you will not be using oil, spray the meat regularly with wine to avoid burning it. When the fillet is golden brown all over, pour in the remaining wine and strawberry juice, turn the heat to low, add salt and pepper to taste, then cover and simmer for 10 minutes.

*5.* At this point, remove the cover and reduce the liquid on high heat. Then, remove from heat, let the fillet cool on a chopping board, and slice. Serve garnished with strawberries and herbs.

# BAKED OMELETTE

*Milk is the most nutritionally complete food for growing children. It contains high doses of calcium, phosphorus, potassium, magnesium and complete proteins. It is ideal for tooth development, and can reduce systolic blood pressure and cardiovascular risks by balancing fat levels in the blood. In low-calorie diets, it can also be effective against obesity. It inhibits the development of diabetes, protects the large intestine against cancer, provides liquids to the body (due to its high water content), and aids mental concentration.*

EASY

**4 servings**
Preparation time: **15 minutes**
Cooking time: **30 minutes**
Calories per portion: **140**

**4 eggs**
**1 3/4 oz. (50 g) fresh ricotta**
**1/2 cup (100 ml) milk**
**1 tbsp parsley, chopped**
**1 bunch herbs (rosemary, parsley, sage and bay leaf)**
**1 courgette**
**1 potato**
**1 red onion**
**1/2 cup (100 ml) vegetable stock**
**Salt**
**Pepper**
**Wine vinegar or balsamic vinegar (optional)**

1. Preheat the oven to 320° F (160° C). Remove all the hard, woody parts from the herbs and finely chop the leaves with a mincing knife or blender.

2. Peel and thinly slice the onion. Peel and dice the potato. Trim, wash and cut the courgette into rounds.

3. Let the vegetables simmer in a non-stick pan for about 10 minutes, spraying with the vegetable stock.

4. Break the eggs into a bowl and add the ricotta, milk, parsley, herbs and vegetables. Season with salt and pepper to taste, then stir.

5. Pour the contents of the bowl into an oven dish lined with greaseproof paper and bake for 20 minutes. Without opening the oven, check that the baked omelette has become firm and, when it is ready, take it out of the oven. When serving, transfer the omelette onto a serving platter and sprinkle with red wine vinegar or balsamic vinegar, both of which will enhance the flavor.

# SALMON FILLET BAKED IN A SALT CRUST

*Whole sea salt not only contains sodium chloride, but also calcium, magnesium, potassium, iron, copper, manganese and zinc, and many other minerals in minor amounts. It is the only truly useful salt in our diet as, given its high nutritional value, it provides greater flavor in smaller concentrations. The amount of salt recommended by FAO (the Food and Agriculture Organization) and WHO (the World Health Organization) is 5-6 grams a day. Whole salt, especially in diets, integrates minerals that would otherwise be difficult to obtain.*

**4 servings**
Preparation time: **10 minutes**
Cooking time: **30 minutes**
Calories per portion: **300**

**1 3/4 lb. (800 g) salmon fillet**
**1 lb. 2 oz. (500 g) whole rock**
**Salt**
**Sage leaves**
**Herb-flavored pepper**

*1.* Preheat the oven to 400° F (200° C).

*2.* Clean, scale and debone the salmon, then wash it and dab it dry with kitchen paper.

*3.* Gently wash and dry the sage.

*4.* Where possible, wrap the salmon flesh in its skin, and cover the exposed parts with sage leaves. This will make it easier to remove the salt when the fish is cooked (keep a few sage leaves aside as garnish).

*5.* Line an oven dish with salt, place the fillet on top and then cover it entirely with another layer of salt. Bake for about 30 minutes.

*6.* Once cooked, remove the salt gently. Place the salmon on a serving platter and garnish with sage leaves. Serve hot. If you wish, you can flavor the dish with a sprinkling of herb-flavored pepper.

# SEAWEED AND PRAWN AVOCADO

*Avocado contains many unsaturated fats and omega-3 fatty acids, which are useful antioxidants in the fight against cancer (especially of the mouth) and vascular diseases. It raises HDL (or "good" cholesterol) and reduces LDL ("bad" cholesterol). It is also rich in vitamin A and E: together with lutein and glutathione, these vitamins serve as excellent antioxidants to prevent the ageing of tissues. Some studies also indicate that avocado performs an antidepressant action and is useful in the fight against Alzheimer's.*

 EASY

**4 servings**
Preparation time: **20 minutes**
Calories per portion: **370**

*1.* Cut the sheet of seaweed into small pieces, and set them aside until ready for use.

*2.* Wash and halve the avocados and remove the stone. Gently spoon some of the pulp from the centre of the fruit into a bowl. Add the soy cream, a pinch of turmeric and the seaweed, then stir.

*3.* Wash the prawns and dip them into a pot of boiling water for 30 seconds, then drain and rinse immediately under cold running water to stop them cooking. Allow them to cool.

*4.* When the prawns are cold, add them to the other ingredients and stir. Season with salt and pepper to taste.

*5.* Spoon some seaweed mixture into the hollow of the avocado halves and add two prawns on top of each. Serve the avocado at room temperature.

**2 avocados**
**8 prawns**
**1 sheet nori seaweed**
**1/4 cup (50 g) soy cream**
**1 tbsp turmeric**
**Salt**
**Pepper**

# PRAWN KEBABS

*Prawns are protein-rich shellfish (approximately 15%). Their fat and sugar content is particularly low, and indeed it is their low calorie count that makes prawns attractive to dieters. They also contain a substance that has recently come under the spotlight in nutraceutics: astaxanthin, a bioflavonoid believed to significantly prevent the ageing of tissues and damage caused by vascular diseases in terms of microcirculation.*

**4 servings**
Preparation time: **10 minutes**
Cooking time: **15 minutes**
Calories per portion: **100**

*1.* Wash the peppers, remove the stalk, seeds and white parts, then chop them into pieces. Peel the onions and cut them into fairly large chunks, so that the concentric leaves do not peel away.

*2.* Wash the prawns and skewer them onto wooden sticks, alternating them with the onion and peppers. Repeat until the all the ingredients are used up.

*3.* Cook the skewers on a hot grill as desired. Spray them with freshly squeezed lemon juice to avoid them from burning.

*4.* Arrange the skewers on individual dishes. Salt and pepper to taste, then serve.

**16 prawns**
**2 red onions**
**1 red bell pepper**
**1 yellow bell pepper**
**2 lemons**
**Salt**
**Pepper**

# TUNA STEAK WITH HERBS

*Tuna is an excellent source of omega-3, protein, potassium, selenium and vitamin B12. It is also a good source of niacin and phosphorus. It is best eaten fresh, so as to avoid losing its antioxidant and anticancer properties through tinning. Numerous studies show its effectiveness against degenerative diseases of the brain, as well as its protective effects on the heart, eyesight and blood pressure. Unfortunately, however, the finest varieties of this fish (such as the bluefin tuna) are endangered.*

**4 servings**
Preparation time: **15 minutes**
Cooking time: **10-15 minutes**
Calories per portion: **210**

1 3/4 lb. (800 g) tuna fillet
14 oz. (400 g) chard stems
10 chive leaves
Soy sauce to taste
Freshly ground pepper
Wasabi (optional)

*1.* Clean and wash the chard stems. Select the best and largest leaves. Discard the white part and keep the green part whole. Cook this in a pot of boiling water for a few minutes, then drain gently. Place the chard leaves on a handy work surface, side by side.

*2.* Overlap the leaves slightly so as to create a sheet, then carefully wrap the tuna steak in it.

*3.* Cook the fillet on a hot non-stick pan or grill for about 10 minutes or so, turning it on all sides so as to cook it evenly.

*4.* Once cooked, remove the tuna from the pan, place it on a chopping board, wait a few minutes for it to cool, and slice it with a very sharp knife.

*5.* Cut the chives into small pieces.

*6.* Serve the slices of fish on individual plates, accompanying them with a bowl of soy sauce flavored with chives, freshly ground pepper and, if you wish, a little wasabi, so that your guests can flavor their dish at will.

# LEMON AND CHILLI SQUID

*Lemon is high in vitamin C. Furthermore, its high mineral and acid content makes it an excellent toning agent, capable of revitalising the entire body. This citrus fruit is a great thirst quencher, as well as performing an effective anticancer and anti-ageing action. Due to its extremely low calorie content, it is ideal in all low-fat diets. Excessive consumption, however, can cause constipation.*

EASY

**4 servings**
Preparation time: **40 minutes**
Cooking time: **10 minutes**
Resting time: **30 minutes**
Calories per portion: **259**

14 oz. (400 g) squid
1 1/3 lbs. (600 g) mussels
14 oz. (400 g) carpet shell clams
4 cockles
2 lemons
4 fresh chilli peppers, medium hot
1 tsp dried chilli pepper, chopped
1 sprig parsley
Salt

1. Soak the mussels, cockles and clams separately in water, with a tablespoon of salt, for about 30 minutes, shaking the water from time to time.

2. Wash the parsley and remove the hard parts. Keep it wrapped in kitchen paper until ready for use. Check the cockles, mussels and clams one by one, tapping them along the slit to ensure they are tightly closed. Discard any open ones. Rinse the molluscs separately and let them drain.

3. Gut the squid and remove the beaks, then wash well. Wash and slice the lemons.

4. Heat the mussels in one non-stick pan and the clams and cockles in another (they have different opening times). Once opened, remove them from heat and let them stand, keeping the pan covered.

5. Cook the squid in a non-stick pan, spraying when needed with the liquid produced by the molluscs. Add the chopped chilli pepper and cook for about 5 minutes. Meanwhile, mince half the parsley.

6. Place the molluscs and the squid in a bowl, salt to taste and add the chopped parsley. Prepare individual portions in bowls or plates, garnishing and flavoring with the lemon slices, the freshly chopped chilli pepper and the remaining parsley. This dish can be served hot or at room temperature, according to your taste.

# BAKED DENTEX FILLET

*Common dentex has very fine meat. It is usually sold farmed, so read the label carefully: extensive farming is a greater guarantee of quality than intensive farming. Common dentex is an excellent source of unsaturated fatty acids and minerals, such as calcium and phosphorus, in addition to vitamin A. Its has complete proteins and, overall, its fat content is quite low.*

**EASY**

**4 servings**
Preparation time: **20 minutes**
Cooking time: **20 minutes**
Calories per portion: **128**

**14 oz. (400 g) dentex fillet**
**4 tomatoes, firm and ripe**
**1 bunch herbs (thyme and parsley)**
**Salt flavored with spices**
**Pepper flavored with spices**
**Salt**
**Pepper**
**1 lemon (optional)**

*1.* Preheat the oven to 350° F (180° C).

*2.* Clean, wash and slice the tomatoes, and drain the excess liquid in a sieve.

*3.* Clean, wash and chop the parsley and thyme, keeping aside some sprigs as garnish.

*4.* Gently wash and dry the dentex fillets with kitchen paper, then remove any bones with tweezers.

*5.* Layer the fillets in a baking dish, alternating them with slices of tomato (keep aside some as garnish). Season with plenty of herbs, then salt and pepper to taste.

*6.* Bake for about 20 minutes. If the fish isn't quite cooked to your liking, leave the baking dish in the oven for a few more minutes.

*7.* Remove from the oven and garnish with the remaining thyme and parsley. Add a few slices of fresh tomato, sprinkle with spice-flavored salt or pepper and, if you wish, drizzle with freshly squeezed lemon juice.

# SEASONED PECORINO CHEESE AND RED CHICORY

*Tuscan Pienza Pecorino cheese has earned the Protected Designation of Origin status (D.O.P.). It comes with a firm, soft or semi-firm texture. It is rich in nutritional properties due to its complete proteins, its easily digestible calcium and its vitamins (A, E and B-complex). It is also a good source of potassium, phosphorus, sodium, calcium and magnesium. It is very effective in the prevention of osteoporosis.*

**EASY**

**4 servings**
Preparation time: **10 minutes**
Cooking time: **15 minutes**
Calories per portion: **185**

14 oz. (400 g) red chicory
10 1/2 oz. (300 g) Tuscan
Pienza Pecorino cheese,
medium aged
4 tbsp (50 g) wildflower honey
4 tbsp (50 g) rose honey
Freshly ground black pepper

*1.* Clean, wash and dry the chicory gently. Cook part of the salad in a non-stick pan for a few minutes, seasoning with salt and pepper to taste. Keep the rest of the chicory aside, wrapped in a damp cloth, until ready for use.

*2.* Discard the rind of the Pecorino and cut the cheese into four. Heat a non-stick pan and, once hot, cook the cheese until a thin crust forms.

*3.* Pour the two types of honey into separate bowls that you will serve with the cheese.

*4.* Once cooked, place the cheese on a platter, over a bed of partly raw and partly cooked chicory, and sprinkle with freshly ground pepper. Serve with the wildflower and rose honey.

SIDE DISHES ARE RICH IN VITAMINS, DIETARY MINERALS, WATER AND FIBRES, ALL OF WHICH KEEP THE DIGESTIVE SYSTEM REGULAR AND PROVIDE A SENSE OF FULLNESS. THEIR CALORIE CONTENT IS GENERALLY VERY LOW, BUT BEWARE OF SAUCES AND CONDIMENTS.

In a low-fat diet, side dishes are almost always made up of vegetables, mushrooms and fruit, valuable foods that can make a real difference, helping us keep our appetite under control, supporting us with their fibre content, and providing a sense of fullness with very few calories. But above all, they allow us to supplement our diet with vitamins and minerals that are often not found in other courses.

Cooking techniques are very important in the preparation of balanced meals. Prolonged exposure to heat can deplete food of its precious nutrients, but steaming, grilling and oven baking are the least harmful cooking methods. Wherever possible, freshly picked foods can often be eaten raw. The ingredients that can be used in side dishes are countless and extremely varied in terms of colour, shape and texture. Season after season, your table will come to life with tomatoes, courgettes, cabbages, carrots, potatoes and many more vegetables besides, which can serve as a main course if accompanied with nuts, cheese or tofu, or if consumed in such quantities as to provide a satisfying sense of fullness. Vegetarians base their entire diet on vegetables, and it is easy to understandable why: even when eaten in large quantities, they do not overload the organs with toxins, residues and saturated fats. When buying them, however, it is important to check where they were grown and whether or not they have been produced respecting the environment. In a low-fat diet, it is possible to prepare light but tasty side dishes accompanying first or second courses or doubling as wonderful appetisers: a plateful of button mushrooms, for example, while rich in nutrients, has fewer than 50 calories,

# SIDE DISHES

provided the are cooked gently and in vegetable stock rather than oil. The same applies to aubergines: grilled, their calorie content is virtually negligible, while particularly tasty when flavored with garlic, turmeric and mint. Courgettes, the diuretic and refreshing vegetable by definition, can be filled to create veritable treasure troves of flavor, or, if small small, firm and seedless, served raw with Parmesan shavings and nuts. Spices, herbs, flavored vinegars and coarse salts are to be considered our precious allies at all times. In addition to their flavor and aroma, they induce a sense of contentment and fullness that is very useful in a low-calorie diet, which can sometimes appear limiting and unappealing. Furthermore, it is advisable to serve side dishes before other more demanding dishes, to aid digestion and give a sense of fullness with very few calories!

# BAKED VEGETABLES
# WITH SOY SAUCE

*Aubergine, a member of the nightshade family, is very rich in water and low in sugar, potassium and fibre. Being low in fat and having a high water content, it is the perfect choice in low-calorie diets. It is a good source of vitamins, especially of the A and C groups. It has a slightly spicy taste, and boasts purifying, diuretic and digestive properties. It also stimulates liver and gallbladder activity.*

**4 servings**
Preparation time: **10 minutes**
Cooking time: **15 minutes**
Calories per serving: **106**

2 courgettes
1 red bell pepper
1 yellow bell pepper
1 green pepper, long
4 round chilli peppers
2 red onions
1 aubergine
4 celery stalks
2 carrots
2 tbsp soy sauce
Salt
Pepper

*1.* Preheat the oven to 400° F (200° C).

*2.* Clean, wash and chop the peppers, celery and aubergine. Trim and wash the courgettes, then cut them into rounds. Peel and slice the onions. Wash the chilli peppers and leave them whole. Peel and trim the carrots, then cut them into rounds.

*3.* Transfer the vegetables into a baking dish, drizzle with soy sauce and bake for 15 minutes.

*4.* During this time, stir the vegetables occasionally to ensure they cook evenly. When cooked, season with salt, bearing in mind that soy sauce is very tasty and that the dish could be perfect as it is. Pepper to taste.

*5.* Serve the vegetables hot or at room temperature as a side dish or even as a starter.

# AUBERGINES WITH MINT AND TURMERIC

*In Ayurvedic medicine, turmeric is used to improve digestion by increasing bile flow, thus aiding the digestion of fats, and speeding up the metabolism. It also boasts effective anti-inflammatory, healing and antibacterial properties.*

**4 servings**
Preparation time: **10 minutes**
Cooking time: **10 minutes**
Resting time: **10 minutes**
Calories per serving: **40**

2 aubergines
1 tbsp turmeric
1 bunch mint
4 cloves of garlic
Salt
Pepper

*1.* Wash and dry the aubergines, then remove the stalks and cut them into wedges.

*2.* Peel and slice the garlic and keep it aside until ready for use.

*3.* Heat a non-stick pan and toast the aubergine slices for about 10 minutes, turning them often, until crispy on the outside but soft and tender on the inside. Remove them from the pan and transfer them into a dish. Salt and pepper to taste.

*4.* Season the aubergine slices with half the sliced garlic, half the turmeric and half the freshly chopped mint, then stir and leave to flavor for about 10 minutes.

*5.* Arrange the vegetables in a serving dish and add the remaining garlic, sprinkle with the remaining turmeric, and decorate with a few mint leaves.

*6.* Serve at room temperature as a side dish or even as a light second course. If you wish to dress the dish with a little oil, add it at the last moment and choose a cold pressed extra virgin olive oil (remember that a spoonful of oil is equivalent to 90 calories).

# TOFU-STUFFED COURGETTES

*Garlic is one of the most interesting bulbs used in cooking due to its ability to underscore and enhance the flavor and aroma of a great variety of dishes. Moreover, it also boasts considerable health benefits, for which it should absolutely not be underestimated! It particular, it helps to keep cholesterol and blood pressure low. Furthermore, it is a natural antibiotic and has mild anti-inflammatory properties.*

MEDIUM

**4 servings**
Preparation time: **10 minutes**
Cooking time: **45 minutes**
Calories per serving: **120**

4 courgettes, round
5 oz. (150 g) tofu
14 oz. (400 g) peeled
tomatoes
2 cloves of garlic
1 white onion
1 bunch basil
Salt
Pepper

1. Preheat the oven to 400° F (200° C). Wash the courgettes, cut their tops off and hollow them out with a teaspoon. Keep the pulp aside in a bowl. Also keep the tops as they will be needed to cover the stuffing.

2. Peel and chop the garlic and onion. Wash and clean the basil.

3. In a non-stick pan, cook the peeled tomatoes with the garlic and onion for about fifteen minutes or until the tomato sauce thickens and reduces by half.

4. Drain and chop the tofu and add it to the courgette pulp. Add the tomato sauce, keeping a few spoonfuls aside, then salt and pepper to taste and mix well.

5. Pour the filling into the courgettes, garnish with a few basil leaves and close them with the tops kept aside.

6. Arrange the courgettes in a baking dish, pour over the remaining tomato sauce and bake for 30 minutes. When the stuffed vegetables have reached the desired consistency, remove them from the oven and serve hot.

# VEGETABLE-STUFFED BAKED TOMATOES

*Parsley is a very popular herb in its native Southern Europe. It contains 50% sugar, 26% protein and 6% water. The rest is made up of fibres and minerals, such as calcium, potassium, sodium, phosphorus, magnesium, iron, zinc, selenium and manganese. Its includes vitamins A, C, E, K and of the B-complex, in addition to being a good source of amino acids and, above all, antioxidant bioflavonoids. The latter can delay cellular ageing and reduce the risk of various types of cancers. Parsley also stimulates gastric activity, thus helping to eliminate trapped wind. It is also an effective tonic and an excellent diuretic.*

**4 servings**
Preparation time: **10 minutes**
Cooking time: **30 minutes**
Resting time: **5 minutes**
Calories per serving: **90**

4 tomatoes
1 courgette
1 aubergine
1 carrot
1 red onion
1 clove of garlic
3/4 oz. (20 g) chopped parsley
1/2 cup (100 ml) vegetable stock
1/2 cup (50 g) breadcrumbs
1 head lettuce as garnish
Salt
Pepper

*1.* Preheat the oven to 400° F (200° C).

*2.* Wash and cut the tomatoes in half, then seed them and allow them to drain upside down on a chopping board.

*3.* Clean, wash and dry the salad gently. Set it aside until ready to use, wrapped in a damp cotton or linen cloth.

*4.* Trim, wash and chop the courgette. Wash and chop the aubergine and carrot. Peel and chop the garlic and onion. Transfer the vegetables into a non-stick pan and cook in vegetable stock for about 10 minutes. Add the chopped parsley, then salt and pepper to taste.

*5.* Spoon the vegetables into the tomatoes, then sprinkle with the breadcrumbs.

*6.* Bake for about 20 minutes, then remove and let cool for 5 minutes.

*7.* When serving, arrange the salad leaves on a serving dish and place the stuffed tomatoes on them.

# GARLIC AND PARSLEY MUSHROOMS

*Mushrooms are generally very popular in low-calorie diets as they are fat free and are rich in proteins and minerals (phosphorus, selenium, potassium and copper). They are also very useful for blood circulation and bone health. Moreover, their extremely high water content (around 99%) makes them very low in calories. They have excellent diuretic properties, and a laxative effect if eaten in large quantities.*

**4 servings**
Preparation time: **10 minutes**
Cooking time: **7 minutes**
Calories per serving: **50**

1 3/4 lb. (800 g) button mushrooms
1 3/4 oz. (50 g) parsley
2 cloves of garlic
1 fresh red chilli pepper
Salt

*1.* Wash the mushrooms as gently as possible and remove the earth and the stem just below the cap. Cut them into two or four, depending on their size.

*2.* Clean, wash and mince the parsley. Peel and chop the garlic.

*3.* Slice the chilli peppers into rounds and add them to the garlic and parsley.

*4.* In a non-stick pan, cook the mushrooms, garlic, parsley and chilli pepper evenly for 5-7 minutes on high heat, stirring continuously.

*5.* While cooking, salt the mushrooms to taste. When they have reached the desired consistency, remove the pan from heat and serve the sautéed mushrooms hot.

# SAUTÉED RED CHICORY
# WITH CHILLI PEPPER AND PINE NUTS

*Pine nuts are high in calories, being made up of 50% fat, and therefore should be used with caution in diets. However, about 85% are unsaturated fats, which have a positive effect on our well-being by improving blood circulation. Pine nuts contain vitamins A, E and B-complex, as well as many essential amino acids. They are also a good source of minerals (phosphorus, copper, selenium and iron).*

**4 servings**
Preparation time: **10 minutes**
Cooking time: **11 minutes**
Calories per serving: **60**

1. Clean, wash, dry and chop the chicory. Clean the green and red chilli peppers, then chop the former and slice the latter. Peel the onion and cut it into thick slices of about 2 mm.

2. In a non-stick pan, lightly toast the pine nuts over medium heat for 2 minutes, stirring continuously, then remove them from the pan and replace them with the onion and a tablespoon of stock. Let the onion soften for 2 minutes and then add the green and red chilli peppers and the salad. Cook the chicory for about 5-7 minutes, stirring with a wooden spoon and spraying, if necessary, with the stock.

3. Halfway through cooking, add salt and pepper to taste.

4. Transfer the ingredients into a serving dish and garnish with pine nuts.

**4 heads red chicory**
**1 red onion**
**3 1/2 oz. (100 g) sweet green chilli pepper, fresh**
**4 red chilli peppers**
**1/2 cup (100 ml) vegetable stock**
**3/4 oz. (20 g) pine nuts**
**Salt**
**Pepper**

# POTATO SALAD WITH PINE NUTS, HERBS, CHILLI PEPPER AND YOGHURT

*Yoghurt can be made from any type of milk and is much more digestible than the source product. It is slightly acid in taste due to its contamination with active cultures, which transform lactose into lactic acid. In addition to the traditional benefits of milk proteins, which are essential for the growth of children, it contains B-complex vitamins. Moreover, the active cultures with which it is made are essential for a healthy digestive system. It also protects and strengthens the autoimmune system, especially during treatment with antibiotics.*

**4 servings**
Preparation time: **10 minutes**
Cooking time: **20 minutes**
Calories per serving: **186**

*1.* Steam the potatoes to the desired consistency (approximately 20 minutes). Once cooked, wait for them to cool, then cut them into wedges without peeling them. Wash the pepper, remove the stalk, seeds and white parts, then cut it into small pieces.

*2.* Remove all the hard, woody parts from the herbs. Finely chop the leaves with a mincing knife or blender, then toast them lightly in a non-stick pan.

*3.* Pour the potatoes, pine nuts, chopped pepper, herbs and yoghurt into a salad bowl and mix well. Add salt and pepper to taste. Serve at room temperature.

1 3/4 lb. (800 g) new potatoes
3/4 oz. (20 g) pine nuts
1/2 cup (100 g) goat's yoghurt
1 sweet red bell pepper, small
1 bunch herbs (thyme, oregano and parsley)
1 tbsp dried chilli pepper, chopped
Salt

# SWEET AND SOUR VEGETABLES

*Wine vinegar is made up of water, amino acids (capable of stimulating the organism's metabolism), vitamins and dietary minerals, such as calcium, potassium, sodium and phosphorus. Consumed regularly, it can be a valuable aid to our well-being. It is also useful to lower cholesterol levels and fight free radicals.*

EASY

**4 servings**
Preparation time: **40 minutes**
Cooking time: **20 minutes**
Calories per serving: **80**

7 oz. (200 g) celery
3 1/2 oz. (100 g) green beans
7 oz. (200 g) pumpkin
14 oz. (400 g) cauliflower
2 carrots
1 fennel
1 yellow bell pepper
1/2 cup (100 ml) white wine vinegar
1/2 cup (100 ml) white wine
1 tbsp sugar
4 bay leaves
10 peppercorns

**For the flavored salt:**
3 1/2 oz. (100 g) sea salt flakes
11/2 tbsp (10 g) turmeric

**For the flavored pepper:**
1 tbsp peppercorns
1 tbsp herbs, chopped (rosemary, oregano, thyme and sage)

1. Place all the vegetables in cold water with a tablespoon of baking soda. When they are clean, rinse them and then leaf, trim or peel them, as need be. Dry them on a clean dish towel and cut them as follows: cut the fennel into four, the green beans into two, the celery into 3/4 inch (2 cm) pieces, the pumpkin into dice, and the cauliflower into florets.

2. To make the flavored salt and pepper, stir the salt and turmeric in one bowl and the mixed herbs and freshly ground pepper in another.

3. Pour about 1 litre of water into a pot and add the vinegar, wine, bay leaf, sugar and peppercorns. Bring to the boil.

4. Start by boiling the carrots, for 2-3 minutes, then remove with a skimmer. Proceed with all the other vegetables, starting with the sweetest and most delicate and ending with the cauliflower, then drain and allow to evaporate.

5. Mix the vegetables in a salad bowl and add the flavored salt and pepper to taste. These sweet and sour vegetables can be stored for several days in the refrigerator, and can also be stored in glass jars in their cooking liquid. A very simple way to sterilise these jars for storage purposes is to cover the vegetables with the cooking liquid, seal the jars tightly and allow them to boil in water, wrapped in cloth, for 5 minutes. Remove them from the pot and let them cool, then wait for a vacuum to form (a slight recess will form in the cap, as if it were sucked inward). Store the jars in a dry, dark place until ready to use.

# SAVOY CABBAGE SALAD
# WITH ANCHOVIES AND GARLIC

*In their natural state (just caught), anchovies are low in calories, being one third made of water, and are rich in calcium, phosphorus, potassium and sodium. In terms of vitamins, they contain niacin, folic acid, retinol and vitamin D. In salted anchovies, however, cholesterol levels double and the sodium content increases exponentially. Despite this, they are a valuable element of our diet, especially in winter.*

**4 servings**
Preparation time: **10 minutes**
Calories per serving: **108**

1 savoy cabbage
(approximately 1 1/3 lbs./600 g)
2 cloves of garlic
1 3/4 oz. (50 g) salted anchovies
1 tbsp red wine vinegar
1 tbsp extra virgin olive oil
Whole table salt

*1.* Clean and wash the cabbage, then cut it into thin strips.

*2.* Peel and chop the garlic.

*3.* Rinse the anchovies lightly (without soaking them) and chop them finely.

*4.* Place the cabbage, anchovies and chopped garlic in a salad bowl. Pour the oil and vinegar into a bowl and mix well, then pour them over the salad and mix to blend the flavors.

*5.* If desired, add salt to taste, but remember that anchovies are a flavorsome fish: taste the cabbage before adding salt, to check whether it is actually necessary. Serve the salad at room temperature. Do not throw out any left over cabbage as, after a few hours or even a whole day, this dish will taste even better.

# COURGETTE SALAD WITH NUTS AND PARMESAN SHAVINGS

*Parmesan is a light cheese made from semi-skimmed milk. It has a fat content of 28% but, despite being of animal origin, over 40% of its fats are unsaturated, and hence highly digestible. Moreover, it is a quick and powerful energy source. The average cholesterol content in 1 3/4 oz. (50 grams) of Parmesan is just 70 milligrams, but it is in any case advisable not use it in great quantities in slimming diets.*

**EASY**

**4 servings**
Preparation time: **10 minutes**
Calories per serving: **90**

4 courgettes, fresh
3/4 oz. (20 g) peanuts
3/4 oz. (20 g) pine nuts
4 tbsp (20 g) Parmesan cheese
Salt
Pepper

*1.* To make sure the courgettes are fresh, buy them with the flower attached. Wash and trim the courgettes, removing the flowers, then cut them into rounds.

*2.* Shell the peanuts and toast them lightly in a non-stick pan (this makes their fat easier to digest) with the pine nuts, for 1-2 minutes, then remove from heat and let cool.

*3.* Make some Parmesan shavings with a potato peeler.

*4.* Pour the sliced courgettes, toasted seeds and half the cheese into a salad bowl. Add salt and pepper to taste, then stir.

*5.* Arrange the salad in individual bowls, sprinkle with the remaining shavings, and serve at room temperature.

# ANCHOVIES AND BELL PEPPERS

*Bell peppers belong to the nightshade family. They are made of 92% water, 1-2% vegetable protein, 2-3% sugar and just 0.2-0.4% fat. As a result they are low in calories, while rich in retinol and vitamins C and A, both useful antioxidants for the prevention of degenerative diseases. They are a good source of fibres, and also include pectin and different types of cellulose. In terms of minerals, they contain potassium and phosphorus. In preparing this dish, it is advisable to choose peppers such as the California Wonder or the Quadrato d'Asti, from which the skin is easily removed, as this can cause indigestion.*

**4 servings**
Preparation time: **10 minutes**
Cooking time: **5 minutes**
Calories per serving: **50**

1 red bell pepper
1 yellow bell pepper
3 1/2 oz. (100 g) salted
anchovies
1/2 cup (100 ml) white wine
vinegar
2 cloves of garlic

1. Peel, wash and cut the peppers into strips.

2. Peel and mince the garlic and keep it aside until ready for use. Wash the anchovies under running water, then dab them dry with kitchen paper and remove the central spine.

3. Bring a pot to the boil with 4 cups (1 litre) of water and the vinegar. Add the pepper strips and let them blanch for 5 minutes, then drain.

4. While the peppers are still hot, use a knife to gently remove the outer skin, then place an anchovy fillet on top of each strip. Roll the pepper strips on themselves and close the parcels with toothpicks. Repeat until all the ingredients are used up.

5. Flavor each parcel with the chopped garlic, and serve. If desired, you can season the peppers with a teaspoon of walnut oil, which goes well with the other ingredients (remember that a spoonful of oil is equivalent to 90 calories).

# MILLET BALLS

*Onions are bulbs made up of a number of concentric leaves. They are used as a base for many recipes, due to their special aroma and considerable taste. They are also considered a natural medication capable of detoxifying and cleansing the body. They are low in calories (26 calories per 100 grams), but rich in potassium, phosphorus and folic acid, and can help keep the digestive system regular.*

**EASY**

**4 servings**
Preparation time: **30 minutes**
Cooking time: **20 minutes**
Resting time: **5 minutes**
Calories per serving: **170**

7 oz. (200 g) millet, precooked
1 red bell pepper, small
2 tbsp (20 g) sunflower and
pumpkin seeds (in total)
1/4 oz. (10 g) chopped parsley
2 eggs
1 onion
1/2 cup (50 g) breadcrumbs
Salt
Pepper
Green cabbage leaves
to garnish

*1.* Preheat the oven to 400° F (200° C) and line a baking sheet with greaseproof paper. Wash the pepper, remove the stalk, seeds and white parts, then chop it finely. Peel and mince the onion.

*2.* Pour the millet into a bowl, then add the bell pepper, sunflower and pumpkin seeds, onion, parsley and eggs. Season with salt and pepper to taste and mix until the mixture is smooth.

*3.* Pour the bread crumbs into a bowl. With your hands, form small balls with the millet mixture, then roll them in the breadcrumbs. Place the balls on a baking sheet and cook for about 20 minutes. Remove from the oven. Let the balls cool at room temperature for 5 minutes, then arrange them on the cabbage leaves, and serve. The dish can be stored in the refrigerator for a day.

DESSERTS CAN CREATE TRULY MAGIC MOMENTS: IT IS WORTHY KEEPING THEM FOR SPECIAL OCCASIONS, AND REPLACING THEM IN EVERYDAY LIFE WITH FRUIT-BASED, BUTTER-FREE SWEETS THAT ARE LOW IN SUGAR AND CALORIES. WHAT'S LOST IN FAT IS GAINED IN COLOUR AND VERVE!

Preparing delicious fat-free desserts is certainly a challenge, because by definition they are a triumph of sugar, butter, cream, chocolate and flour. We cannot eliminate flour and eggs, but we can drastically reduce sugar (replacing it with honey or fructose) and use yoghurt instead of cream. And lo! You have a whole variety of ingredients for wonderful, low-calorie cakes.

We can play with colours, beauty and fragrance to prepare satisfying and intriguing desserts, even if we replace cream with delicious home made vanilla yoghurt, or if we serve a slice of butter-free apple pie, whose creamy texture and cinnamon scent will put butter right out of our heads. Of course, in a low-fat diet desserts can drive up the calorie count and lead us astray with regards to our goals. But a slice of home made cocoa cake at breakfast – perhaps not every day, but in moderation – is perfectly acceptable. We should learn to make a habit of eating desserts in the morning, and never after a meal, to avoid adding more and more calories and slowing down our digestion. One of the most common mistakes is to eat a lot at dinnertime, thinking that we can finally put our feet up and indulge in the pleasures of the palate that have had to be put on the back burner throughout the day. But in so doing we fill ourselves up just before going to bed, and in the stillness of the night all this energy unfortunately turns to fat! While dieting, classic desserts can be replaced with visually appealing fruit dishes, for example replacing ice cream with sorbets. We can prepare our own jam, using very little sugar, and only cane sugar at that. We should not forget that, if it is true that by reducing fats we reduce our

# DESSERTS

calorie intake, then it is also true that to achieve well-being, sugar must also be significantly reduced. So let's open the door to vegetable creams, such as those of soy or oats, and ricotta cheese in the place of cream. And then there are lots of fruit, preferably those in season, that can be eaten fresh, cooked, or puréed with yoghurt or ice, depending on the time of year. Pineapple, for example, in addition to being cool and refreshing, can help reduce the fat ingested. New dietary studies certainly put the spotlight on fats, but also on the harmful effects of too much sugar, and the fact that it creates a slight dependency. Giving up on a part of the pleasures of life clearly requires strength of mind, but when we decide to indulge in a slice of cake we should do it with joy, and without guilt, and then try to keep light the following meal, to ensure the overall calorie count does not soar out of control!

# PINEAPPLE MILLE-FEUILLE

*Pineapple is a fruit rich in bromelain, capable of aiding the digestion of proteins, and can be used as an anti-inflammatory and to reduce the sense of swelling given by water retention. It is also a good source of vitamin C, which is useful in strengthening the immune system. Its fibres increase our sense of fullness, and indeed, not surprisingly, pineapple is often recommended in low-calorie diets.*

MEDIUM

**4 servings**
Preparation time: **50 minutes**
Resting time: **30 minutes**
Calories per serving: **210**

1. Peel the pineapple and cut it into two width wise. Cut the larger part into very thin slices (preferably with a slicer) and blend the other half.

2. Pour the mixture into a bowl, add the sugar, sorbet and cream, then stir the ingredients until creamy soft and smooth. Process in the ice cream maker for 30 minutes, then store in the freezer until ready for use.

3. Coarsely chop half the pine nuts and set the rest aside as garnish. Clean, wash and gently dry the blueberries with kitchen paper.

4. Make up the dessert, alternating slices of fresh pineapple with cream and chopped pine nuts. Garnish with the remaining nuts and blueberries. Store the mille-feuille in the freezer. Keep at room temperature for about 10 minutes before serving.

1 pineapple (about 1 kg)
3 1/2 oz. (100 g) pineapple sorbet
1/2 cup (100 g) soy cream
1/3 cup (50 g) icing sugar
3/4 oz. (20 g) pine nuts
1 punnet blueberries

# STUFFED PEACHES

*Chocolate is a concentrate of natural stimulants – caffeine, theobromine, serotonin, tryptophan and phenylethylamine – and is considered the good mood food par excellence! Moreover, its excellent antioxidant properties should not be underestimated: it is rich in precious polyphenols and it is believed that, especially dark chocolate, is effective against vascular diseases and for the prevention of cancer. Furthermore, it is thought to fight brain damage caused by ageing.*

MEDIUM

**4 servings**
Preparation time: **20 minutes**
Cooking time: **30 minutes**
Calories per serving: **135**

4 peaches
40 g amaretto biscuits
1/4 oz. (10 g) almonds
2 egg yolks
2 tbsp cane sugar
2 tbsp (20 g) bitter cocoa powder

*1.* Preheat the oven to 425° F (220° C). In a mortar, finely pound the amaretto biscuits and almonds separately.

*2.* In a bowl, beat the egg yolks with the sugar, then add the cocoa and the ground amaretto biscuits. Stir until the mixture is smooth.

*3.* Wash and cut the peaches in half, and remove the stone. Gently scoop out part of the pulp with a spoon in order to be able to stuff the fruits.

*4.* Spoon the cocoa mixture into the peaches and sprinkle them with the chopped almonds.

*5.* Arrange the peach halves on a baking sheet, propping them up against one another so that they don't topple over while cooking. Bake for about 25-30 minutes.

*6.* When cooked, remove the baking sheet from the oven and let the peaches cool a few minutes before serving. This dessert is great both hot (although not just out of the oven!) and at room temperature.

# STRAWBERRY, BLUEBERRY AND REDCURRANT PANCAKES

*Redcurrants are made up of 80% water, while the remaining 20% is made up of dietary fibres, carbohydrates, proteins and sugars. They contain various minerals (calcium, iron, potassium, sodium, copper, zinc and phosphorus), as well as vitamin A, C and K and some B vitamins. They also contain bioflavonoids with anti-inflammatory and antioxidant properties. Recently, they have been discovered to contain substances with remarkable antihistamine properties, useful in the fight against allergies, and in particular respiratory diseases such as asthma, hay fever and other pollen allergies.*

MEDIUM

**4 servings**
Preparation time: **20 minutes**
Cooking time: **10 minutes**
Calories per serving: **354**

**For the pancakes:**
**2 eggs**
**2 cups (500 ml) milk**
**1 cup (150 g) wheat meal**

**For the filling:**
**3 1/2 oz. (100 g) redcurrants**
**3 1/2 oz. (100 g) blueberries**
**7 oz. (200 g) strawberries**
**1/2 cup (100 g) soy cream,**
**whipped**

1. Wash the blueberries and redcurrants. Clean, wash and chop the strawberries. Put all the fruits in a bowl.

2. Break the eggs into a bowl, then add the milk and flour. Beat using an electric mixer until the mixture is smooth and free of lumps.

3. Grease a 10 inch (25 cm) non-stick pan with kitchen paper soaked in oil, then ladle in some mixture. Move the pan around so as to cover the bottom with a thin layer of mixture and let it cook (this should take less than a minute). Once cooked, the pancake will come away easily from the pan: turn it over and allow it to cook on the other side. Repeat until all the mixture is used up, arranging the pancakes in a dish, one on top of the other.

4. When serving, make up the dessert, distributing some whipped cream and fruit on each pancake. In serving the pancakes, you can give free rein to your imagination: for example, you can roll them up, fold them in half or serve the filling apart.

# FIG AND PEACH BREAD PUDDING

*Peaches are native to China, and widespread in Europe. They are made up of around 90% water. In terms of minerals, they mainly contain potassium, but also iron, calcium, phosphorus and sodium. They are rich in vitamin A, but above all in vitamins C, E and K. Their many fibres and high water content make them ideal in low-calorie diets. The detoxifying and cleansing properties of peaches make them great for the skin and to treat gastrointestinal diseases.*

EASY

**4 servings**
Preparation time: **25 minutes**
Cooking time: **30 minutes**
Calories per serving: **355**

**For the dough:**
3 1/2 oz. (100 g) white bread, stale
3/4 cup plus 1 tbsp (200 ml) milk
1/3 cup (50 g) potato starch
1 egg
1/2 cup (100 g) yoghurt
2 tbsp cane sugar
2 drops lemon essence
1 tbsp baking soda

**To garnish:**
6 figs
1 peach
1 tbsp brown cane sugar

1. Preheat the oven to 350°F (180° C). Wash the figs and the peach and cut them into wedges, without peeling them.

2. Cut the bread into small pieces and let it soak in milk until soft and easily to work, then squeeze it as much as possible and blend it to obtain an almost creamy mixture.

3. Add the potato starch and mix well. Add the egg, sugar and lemon essence, then mix again.

4. In a bowl, pour the yoghurt and sieve in the baking soda, then mix well with a whisk. When the mixture begins to rise, pour it into the bowl with the bread and stir well until smooth and free of lumps.

5. Line a baking tin with greaseproof paper and pour in the mixture. Arrange the fruit wedges on top, pressing down gently with your fingers to incorporate them into the dough, then sprinkle with brown cane sugar and put the tin in the oven.

6. Bake the cake for about 30 minutes, then test to see if it is cooked by skewering it with a toothpick: if it comes out clean, the cake is ready. Remove it from the oven and let it cool at room temperature, otherwise let it cook for another 5 minutes.

# MIXED BERRY SMOOTHIE

*Soy yoghurt is made from soy milk, and therefore is suitable for those suffering from a milk protein intolerance and in diets aimed at reducing animal fats and cholesterol. Like all soybean by-products, it is cholesterol-free, and is an excellent source of fibre and protein, with a low intake of fats. It is also rich in calcium, potassium, phosphorus and folic acid.*

**EASY**

**4 servings**
Preparation time: **10 minutes**
Calories per serving: **180**

300 g strawberries
7 oz. (200 g) blueberries
1 cup (200 g) soy yoghurt
3/4 cup plus 1 tbsp (200 ml) soy milk
10 ice cubes (optional)

1. Keep a few strawberries aside as garnish, then clean the rest, removing the stem, and wash and chop them   into small pieces. Wash the blueberries separately and let them drain in a strainer. Prepare two skewers per person, alternating strawberries and blueberries. Keep them in a cool place until ready to garnish the glasses.

2. Put the chopped strawberries into the blender, add half the milk and blend for about 2 minutes or until the ingredients are well mixed. Pour the mixture into a bowl and mix in half the yoghurt with a small whisk.

3. Make another smoothie with the blueberries. If you are preparing this smoothie in the summer and want to make a thirst-quenching drink, you can add some ice: in addition to diluting it, it will make the drink particularly light and refreshing.

4. Prepare the smoothie a few minutes before serving, so that the beneficial properties of its ingredients are not lost by oxidation.

5. When serving, half fill the glasses with some strawberry smoothie and top this with an equivalent dose of blueberry smoothie. To create two separate layers, slowly pour each smoothie onto the inverted side of a spoon to slow down the rate of flow. Decorate the smoothie with the fruit skewers and serve.

# PEACH AND STRAWBERRY
# JAM TARTS

*Unlike refined sugar, whole cane sugar is not only a source of energy due to fast acting carbohydrates, but also of vitamins, minerals and proteins. It is much easier to digest than white sugar and does not overload the pancreas, therefore acting as a great aid to preventing type-2 diabetes in susceptible individuals. Although it is fat free, it is best not to overindulge in it: an excessive intake may stimulate the formation of endogenous fats.*

MEDIUM

**4 servings**
Preparation time: **35 minutes**
Cooking time: **50 minutes**
Calories per serving: **339**

**For the tarts:**
1 cup (150 g) white flour
1/3 cup (50 g) potato starch
1 tbsp sugar
2 eggs
2 tbsp oil
1/4 cup (50 ml) milk
Butter spray

**For the jam:**
2 yellow peaches
7 oz. (200 g) strawberries
2 tbsp cane sugar

**To garnish:**
1 punnet redcurrants
10 strawberries, small

1. Preheat the oven to 400° F (200° C) and grease four moulds with butter spray.

2. To prepare the jam, clean the fruit and chop it coarsely, then cook it with the sugar in a saucepan on low heat. Press the fruit pieces lightly with a fork and cook for about 30 minutes, stirring regularly with a wooden spoon.

3. Place the flour, sugar, eggs and oil on a rolling board. Knead delicately until the dough is smooth. If it seems too dry, add a few tablespoons of milk. With a rolling pin, roll out the dough to a thickness of about a quarter of an inch and cut out discs of the size of the moulds you are using.

4. Place the discs in the moulds, pressing lightly with your fingers to make them take the shape of the moulds. Add the jam, then use any leftover strips of dough to decorate the tarts. Bake for about 20 minutes.

5. Once cooked, remove them from the oven, let them cool, and garnish with bunches of redcurrants, then sprinkle with icing sugar. Serve with the remaining strawberries.

# CINNAMON APPLE CAKE

*In addition to being a traditional Christmas cake seasoning, cinnamon is well known and appreciated for its digestive properties. Its trypsin content helps break down fat. Furthermore, cinnamon performs an anti-fermentation and antiseptic action. It is also able to lower blood sugar levels, and is believed to curb appetite.*

**4 servings**
Preparation time: **15 minutes**
Cooking time: **30 minutes**
Calories per serving: **280**

2 cups (250 g) flour
2 tbsp (50 g) acacia honey
2 eggs
1/2 cup (100 ml) milk
1 sachet baking powder
2 red Fuji apples
1 tsp cinnamon
powder
1 tbsp icing sugar

*1.* Preheat the oven to 350°F (180° C) and line a rectangular roasting pan (approximately 6 inches by 10) with greaseproof paper.

*2.* Pour the flour, eggs, milk and honey into a metal bowl. Stir with an electric mixer, until smooth and without lumps.

*3.* Add half the cinnamon and the baking powder, then stir again: when thoroughly blended, pour the mixture into the pan. Wash the apples and cut them into wedges, then incorporate them into the mixture to decorate the surface. Sieve the remaining cinnamon onto the cake and bake for about 30 minutes.

*4.* Test to see if it is cooked by skewering it with a toothpick: if it comes out clean, the cake is ready. Remove it from the oven and let it cool at room temperature, otherwise increase the temperature and let it cook for another 5 minutes.

*5.* When cool, remove the greaseproof paper, cut the cake into pieces and sprinkle with icing sugar before serving. This is a classical apple cake, perfect for breakfast or as an afternoon snack. It can be served at room temperature or heated up briefly in the oven, to bring out its scent.

# FRUIT CHESSBOARD

*Watermelon is a large water-rich fruit (up to 94%) that is high in fibres and low in proteins, making it very suitable for low calorie diets. It is also a source of minerals and vitamins (A, C, PP, B1 and B2). Like tomatoes, its red colour is due to the presence of lycopenes, excellent antioxidants with anti-cancer properties, especially of the prostate and breast. Its seeds have considerable laxative, diuretic and cleansing properties, which help the liver and fight cellulite. In statistical terms, those who are allergic to aspirin may also be allergic to watermelon. Furthermore, many people find it hard to digest.*

EASY

**4 servings**
Preparation time: **15 minutes**
Calories per serving: **55**

**For the chessboard:**
**1 kg watermelon**
**14 oz. (400 g) pineapple**

**To garnish:**
**1 kiwi**
**1 bunch of small white grapes**

1. Remove the watermelon seeds, rind and white parts, then cut the pulp into rectangles of about 1 inch x 1 inch x 0.5 inch. Keep aside half the pulp to prepare the juice that will be served with the chessboard.

2. Clean, peel and core the pineapple, and cut it into rectangles of the same size as the watermelon, calculating about four or five rectangles of pineapple and as many of watermelon for each serving.

3. Purée the watermelon pulp and pour the mixture into a jug.

4. Wash the grapes and kiwi, then cut the latter into thin slices. Use four toothpicks to prepare some fruit skewers with which to decorate the chessboard. Skewer each toothpick with a grape, a slice of kiwi and then another grape.

5. Arrange the watermelon and pineapple rectangles on individual plates, alternating them to form a chessboard. Garnish the dessert by inserting a fruit skewer into the central block of each chessboard, and serve with the watermelon juice, to which you can add some ice cubes just before serving.

# CHOCOLATE AND ORANGE CAKE

*Oranges are rich in vitamins C and of the B complex. They rapidly compensate for the loss of dietary salts, in particular potassium and magnesium, and are therefore very suitable to regain strength during convalescence, physical strain and colds. They also contain calcium, zinc, copper and iron, as well as many polyphenols with fast-acting antioxidant activity, making them an effective anti-ageing food.*

MEDIUM

**4 servings**
Preparation time: **20 minutes**
Cooking time: **30 minutes**
Calories per serving: **229**

**1 cup (120 g) white flour**
**1/3 cup (50 g) potato starch**
**4 tbsp (30 g) bitter cocoa powder**
**1 cup (200 g) low-fat natural yoghurt**
**2 tbsp cane sugar**
**1 tsp baking soda**
**2 eggs**
**2 oranges**

1. Preheat the oven to 350° F (180° C). Line a rectangular baking tin with greaseproof paper.

2. Squeeze the juice of an orange.

3. Pour the flour and cocoa into a bowl and mix well. In another bowl, beat the eggs and sugar until creamy, then fold in the flour and cocoa, and stir in the orange juice.

4. Wash and dry the remaining orange and cut it into thin slices.

5. Pour the yoghurt into a container and sieve in the baking soda. Mix well, and when the mixture starts to rise, add it to the other ingredients. Mix well until smooth and free of lumps.

6. Pour the mixture into the tin and decorate the surface with the orange slices. Bake and cook for about 30 minutes.

7. When cooked, remove from the oven and let the cake cool at room temperature before turning it out. Serve at room temperature.

# LAYERED MOUSSE

*Dark chocolate contains a high percentage of beneficial antioxidants (polyphenols) and minerals such as magnesium, potassium, phosphorus, calcium and iron. It contains theobromine, which stimulates the nervous system, promoting concentration and mental alertness. However, dark chocolate is high in calories (542 calories per 100 grams), and, as it is a stimulant, it is best avoided in children's diets, especially in the evening.*

**4 servings**
Preparation time: **20 minutes**
Cooking time: **30 minutes**
Resting time: **2 hours**
Calories per serving: **275**

1. For the milk mousse, bring the milk to the boil with the honey. Remove from heat, add the agar-agar and let it melt, mixing with a whisk. Leave to cool out of the fridge.

2. For the chocolate mousse, melt the dark chocolate on a double boiler, and in the meantime heat the milk. When the chocolate has melted, pour it into the milk and whisk until smooth. Half fill the glasses with the chocolate mixture, then let it cool in the freezer for 10 minutes. Take it out of the freezer and pour the milk mixture over the chocolate.

3. Put the glasses in the refrigerator until the mousses have thickened. Just before serving, sprinkle the glasses with chocolate shavings obtained by scraping the dark chocolate for the garnish with a knife.

**For the milk mousse:**
**1 3/4 cup (400 ml) milk**
**1/8 oz. (5 g) agar-agar**
**2 tbsp (30 g) acacia honey**

**For the chocolate mousse:**
**5 oz. (150 g) dark chocolate**
**3/4 cup plus 1 tbsp (200 ml) milk**

**To garnish:**
**3/4 oz. (20 g) dark chocolate in a single block**

# VANILLA YOGHURT

*Vanilla is a sweet spice with an intense aroma, extracted from an orchid variety with large yellow flowers. It is native to Mexico, but nowadays is also grown in Africa and Asia. Vanillin, the primary component of the extract of the vanilla bean, has antiseptic and digestive properties, and is traditionally considered an aphrodisiac. Recent studies also show that it has beneficial effects on the nervous system, acting as an antidepressant.*

MEDIUM

**4 servings**
Preparation time: **20 minutes**
Cooking time: **4 hours and 20 minutes**
Calories per serving: **176**

1. Preheat the oven to 120° F (50° C).

2. In a heavy-based stainless steel pot, boil the milk with the vanilla for about 20 minutes on low heat, stirring continuously with a wooden spoon to avoid burning.

3. Allow the milk to cool, remove the vanilla pod and, when the liquid reaches 100° F (40° C), put it into an oven-proof sealable container. Add the yoghurt and stir to blend thoroughly, then close the container and bake for 4 hours.

4. After this time, the yoghurt will have thickened. You can enjoy it warm, or let it cool in the refrigerator and serve it cold.

**4 cups (1 l) full-fat milk**
**1/2 cup (100 g) natural yoghurt**
**1 vanilla pod**

# LEMON SORBET WITH POMEGRANATE

*Pomegranate is the fruit of the* Punica granatum. *Its seeds are diuretic, aid digestion and have astringent properties. The fruit has a large quantity of soft seeds embedded in a spongy, astringent membrane. The seeds are low in calories (about 63 per 100 grams), are made up of about 80% water, and are rich in potassium, vitamin C and folic acid.*

**4 servings**
Preparation time: **10 minutes**
Resting time: **2 hours**
Calories per serving: **200**

5 lemons
**7 oz. (200 g) brown cane sugar**
**1 pomegranate**
**1 tbsp edible flower petals**

*1.* Squeeze the lemons and strain the juice. Boil the sugar with 1 1/4 cup (300 ml) of water for 2 minutes, then stir, remove from heat and allow to cool.

*2.* When the sugar syrup is cool, add it to the lemon juice, mix, and transfer it into an ice cream maker. Process for about 30 minutes, then transfer the sorbet into the freezer. If you do not have an ice cream maker, place the ingredients in a sealable container and place it in the freezer. Every 20 minutes, take it out and stir the sorbet, so that it does not freeze completely. Repeat for 2 hours or until the texture is firm. At this point, take an electric mixer and process the sorbet for 5 minutes, then put it back into the freezer for a few minutes.

*3.* Clean the pomegranate, peeling away the rind and the inner white papery skin covering the seeds. Set aside the seeds until ready to use.

*4.* Transfer the sorbet into glasses and sprinkle with pomegranate seeds and the edible petals. Serve at once.

# STUFFED MUFFINS

*Common and durum wheat belong to two different species of the grass family. Common wheat flour, a white, almost impalpable powder, is ideal for dough, and is also used for fresh pasta. However, it has fewer proteins than durum wheat flour, and absorbs less water. It contains easily digestible starch, but it is best not to overindulge in it in low-calorie diets.*

MEDIUM

**4 servings**
Preparation time: **20 minutes**
Cooking time: **20 minutes**
Calories per serving: **250**

**For the muffins:**
2 tbsp low fat natural yoghurt
2/3 cup (80 g) common wheat flour
1/3 cup (80 g) brown cane sugar
1 tsp baking soda
1/4 cup (50 ml) milk
1 egg

To garnish:
1/2 cup (100 g) soy cream, whipped
3/4 oz. (20 g) almonds

1. Preheat the oven to 350° F (180° C) and grease a muffin tin.

2. In a bowl, mix the flour and milk. In another, beat the egg with the sugar until creamy, then fold in the flour until smooth and free of lumps.

3. Pour the yoghurt into a bowl and sieve in the baking soda, then stir. When the mixture begins to rise, pour it into the flour and mix the ingredients until thoroughly blended.

4. When you have a smooth, lump-free mixture, pour it into the muffin tin and bake for about 20 minutes.

5. Meanwhile, grind the almonds in a mortar, keeping a few aside, whole, as garnish.

6. When the muffins are ready, remove them from the oven and leave them to cool, then turn them out. Flavor them with whipped cream and the whole and ground almonds, then serve at room temperature.

IS IT POSSIBLE TO PREPARE FAT-FREE SAUCES, AND SEASONINGS THAT ARE TASTY YET LIGHT AND EASY TO DIGEST? THIS CHALLENGE CAN BE OVERCOME BY REPLACING CREAMS AND SAUCES WITH FLAVORED VINEGARS, CHILLI PEPPER, HERBS, SPICES AND SEEDS RICH IN OMEGA-3.

But what sort of cuisine has no sauces? A dull and predictable one. Grilled chicken breast would simply be white meat, and steamed vegetables would have the appeal of a prison sentence. A teaspoon of tomato and chili pepper sauce, instead, opens up a world of colour, and an unexpected kaleidoscope of flavors: sour, fresh, spicy, savoury... But at what price? And with the addition of how many calories?

Very few, as it happens. No one ever said that sauces can only be prepared with oil, butter or lard. Vegetables are extremely flavorsome, adding a dash of taste to otherwise insipid dishes. You might think that sauces are the most affected by a low-fat diet. What springs to mind are mayonnaise, pasta and bruschetta sauces, various basil or caper pestos, and cream: reducing the calories in seasonings while maintaining their flavor would seems to be virtually impossible.

And yet, we have tried to do just that, for example using ricotta cheese mixed with eggs and parsley. The result is a delicious cream sauce, an ideal accompaniment for steamed vegetables and croutons. In the caper pesto, we have replaced oil with Passito wine, thus combining two flavorsome ingredients to create an irresistible sauce that will appeal to all caper lovers.

The sweet wine, tangy capers and aromatic wild fennel come together to produce a delicious paste to be spread on bread or used to season pasta. With the help of soy and oatmeal cream, we have prepared sauces that would be completely off limits if seasoned with oil or cream. "But the flavor changes". Yes, that's a legitimate consideration. The taste is no doubt different, and the

# SAUCES AND DRESSINGS

palate must get used to different textures. Just as it needs to train to detect the fat in nuts and in sesame seeds, for example. Initially you may not taste much, but after a few days the need for rich flavors at all costs will subside, enabling your taste buds to embark on an innovative journey.

We generally choose the foods we are most accustomed to, that we like most and make us feel satisfied, without thinking about their effects on us. There are plenty of theories on healthy eating, but any truly healthy diet should be nutritionally complete. When we find ourselves faced with the need to change our usual eating habits, it is worth turning to new flavors and different approaches to food, discovering often surprising textures and combinations. You may even find that low-fat meals teach you to follow the needs of your body rather than merely of your palate!

# HERB AND SPICE SALTS

*Coarse sea salts are free of calories, salt more effectively and can be used in smaller quantities. Nowadays, as we are all overloaded with salt due to the consumption of tinned and ready foods, it would be best to avoid using pure refined salt. Moreover, coarse salt contains many minerals that benefit the metabolism and act as antioxidants.*

EASY

**4 servings**
Preparation time: **5 minutes**
Calories per serving: **0**

1 3/4 oz. (50 g) white Fiore di Sale salt
1 3/4 oz. (50 g) black salt
3 1/2 oz. (100 g) grey salt
1 3/4 oz. (50 g) red salt
5 tbsp (50 g) flax seeds
5 1/2 tbsp (50 g) light sesame seeds
3/4 oz. (20 g) dried chilli pepper
1 tbsp (10 g) turmeric
1 3/4 oz. (50 g) dried oregano
3/4 oz. (20 g) parsley

1. Clean, wash and dry the parsley, let it dry in the oven at 425° F (220° C) for about 5-10 minutes, then crumble it with your hands.

2. Repeat with the oregano and add it to the parsley.

3. Lightly toast the flax seeds in a non-stick pan, shaking often to prevent them from burning. After 2 minutes, remove from heat and let cool.

4. Take six containers and fill them as follows: the first with Fiore di Sale salt mixed with flax seeds, the second with black salt mixed with sesame seeds, the third with half the grey salt mixed with dried chopped chilli pepper, the fourth with the other half of the grey salt mixed with turmeric, the fifth with red salt and the last with oregano mixed with parsley.

5. For greater visual impact, serve the containers along with jars of powders and spices. This system will allow you to use less salt and flavor those seemingly unappetizing low-calorie dishes.

# RICOTTA CREAM SAUCE WITH EGGS AND PARSLEY

*Ricotta is rich in whey protein and energy. It is low in fat, and hence fairly low in calories, provided it is not combined with cream or whole milk. Its fat content varies greatly, from 5% to 15%, depending on the type of ricotta. For this reason, it would be preferable to know its fat content precisely and to choose the lightest ricotta possible.*

EASY

**4 servings**
Preparation time: **5 minutes**
Calories per serving: **113**

1. Clean and wash the parsley. Keep a few sprigs aside as garnish, and mince the rest with a mincing knife or blender.

2. Pour the egg yolks into a bowl and fold in the ricotta cheese and parsley. Salt and pepper to taste, stirring until creamy, smooth, and free of lumps.

3. Transfer the mixture into a gravy boat and garnish with a few parsley leaves.

4. Serve the ricotta cheese with breadsticks, or use it to flavor vegetables, pasta, rice or boiled fish. The sauce is also an excellent dip for raw vegetables, for a light yet tasty appetiser.

**7 oz. (200 g) fresh ricotta**
**2 egg yolks, fresh**
**3/4 oz. (20 g) parsley**
**Salt**
**Pepper**

# CAPER AND ALMOND PESTO

*Capers are the flowers buds of the perennial plant by the same name. They are a good source of protein, vitamins A, E, K and B-complex, and minerals such as iron, copper, manganese and magnesium. As they are often preserved in salt, it is important to soak them in water, rinsing them repeatedly. They stimulate the appetite, aid digestion, help reduce fluid retention and have diuretic properties.*

EASY

**4 servings**
Preparation time: **15 minutes**
Calories per serving: **100**

7 oz. (200 g) Pantelleria
capers preserved in salt
1 3/4 oz. (50 g) almonds
1/2 cup (100 ml) Passito wine
from Pantelleria
1 bunch wild fennel
Freshly ground black pepper

1. Soak the capers in cold water for at least 10 minutes, changing the water several times. Drain them of any excess liquid, pressing them in a strainer, then chop them with a mincing knife on a wooden chopping board.

2. Clean, wash, dry and mince the wild fennel.

3. Finely grind the almonds in a mortar, keeping some, chopped, as garnish.

4. Put all the ingredients in a bowl and spoon in the Passito wine, adding as much as can be absorbed by the other ingredients. Season the pesto with a generous sprinkling of pepper, then stir again and transfer it into a gravy boat, garnishing with some chopped almonds. The capers should provide enough salt for the entire dish. The sauce is excellent on pasta or spread on slices of toasted bread. Its ability to stimulate the appetite makes it a perfect appetiser. It can be stored in the refrigerator for a few days.

# SPICY CHICKPEA CREAM SAUCE

*Paprika is obtained by grinding different types of dried chilli. Native to Central and South America, it is used extensively in North America. In Europe, it is particularly popular in Hungary. It has antiseptic and digestive properties, and is also useful for its antioxidant bioflavanoids. Moreover, it is rich in vitamins A and C and in minerals.*

MEDIUM

**4 servings**
Soaking time: **8 hours**
Preparation time: **10 minutes**
Cooking time: **2 hours**
Calories per serving: **186**

**7 oz. (200 g) dried chickpeas**
**1/2 cup (100 ml) chickpea cooking liquid**
**1 white onion**
**2 sprigs fresh rosemary**
**2 tsp paprika**
**2 tsp curry**
**Salt**
**Pepper**

1. Peel and thinly slice the onion. Clean a sprig of rosemary, removing the hard parts, and chop the leaves finely.

2. Soak the chickpeas in water for 8 hours, then drain and rinse several times. Boil with the rosemary and onion for about 2 hours.

3. After cooking, transfer the chickpeas into a blender using a skimmer, and keep the liquid.

4. Keep a spoonful of chickpeas aside and blend the rest, if necessary moistening them with the cooking liquid. Blend until the mixture is smooth.

5. Put the cream in a bowl, then salt and pepper to taste. Add the paprika and curry powder, keeping a teaspoon of each aside as garnish. Add the whole chickpeas and stir well.

6. Transfer the sauce into a serving dish, sprinkle with the spices and garnish with the remaining rosemary. This cream sauce is a great starter served with croutons, bread or breadsticks, and goes very well with vegetables or pulses.

# GREEN SAUCE WITH PINE NUTS

*Mint is a herb made up primarily of water, fibres, proteins and carbohydrates. In terms of minerals, it contains calcium, potassium, magnesium, copper, manganese, sodium and phosphorus. It also contains a considerable amount of vitamins A, C, D and B-complex, and plenty of amino acids, such as arginine, aspartic acid, glutamic acid, alanine, leucine, glycine, proline, serine and valine. While mint stimulates the gastric juices and aids digestion, it is not suitable for people suffering from gastric and duodenal ulcers.*

EASY

**4 servings**
Preparation time: **10 minutes**
Calories per serving: **93**

*1.* Gently wash and dry the basil and mint, removing the hard parts and keeping only the leaves (keep a few aside as garnish). Mince the herbs with a mincing knife or blender. Gently crush the pine nuts in a mortar, keeping some aside as garnish.

*2.* Grate the Parmesan cheese and pour it into a bowl, together with the oatmeal cream, crushed pine nuts and chopped herbs. Season with salt and pepper to taste. Mix well until the mixture is smooth.

*3.* Transfer the mixture into a gravy boat and garnish with the remaining herbs and pine nuts. Serve as a sauce for pasta, rice or chicken breast. This sauce is also great to season salads and vegetables, both cooked and raw, and is perfect on croutons, focaccia and home made bread.

2 1/2 oz. (70 g) basil
3/4 oz. (20 g) mint
3/4 oz. (20 g) pine nuts
1/2 cup (100 g) oatmeal cream
3 tbsp (20 g) Parmesan cheese
Salt
Pepper

# FLAVORED VINEGAR

*Bay leaf contains digestive, neurotrophic and toning substances capable of calming the nervous system. It also stimulates the digestive system, making food more digestible, and can help eliminate wind. It also has analgesic properties, ideal for those who suffer from muscle cramps or sprains.*

**Ingredients for 1 litre**
Preparation time: **10 minutes**
Resting time: **1 week to 10 days**
Calories per serving: **4**

1. Pour the vinegar into a container that can be closed but not sealed.

2. Peel the garlic and onion and cut them into rings. Wash, dry and slice the chilli peppers. Wash and dry the bay leaves.

3. Pour the juniper berries, the black pepper and the other ingredients into the bowl with the vinegar.

4. Allow to rest in the dark for a week to 10 days, stirring from time to time. Then, strain the flavored vinegar, pour it into a bottle and cap. With its perfumes and aromatic flavor, this seasoning enhances the taste of salads, omelettes, steamed vegetables, cereals and pulses.

4 cups (1 l) red wine vinegar
2 onions
4 cloves of garlic
10 bay leaves
20 juniper berries
20 black peppercorns
4 chilli peppers, fresh

# TOMATO SAUCE
# WITH PARSLEY AND CRUNCHY BREAD

*Toast is bread from which the moisture evaporates as it heats: 3 1/2 oz. (100 grams) of fresh bread correspond to 2 3/4 oz. (85 grams) of toasted bread. Be careful, therefore, not to eat too many dried products, because, while appetizing, they are deceptively high in calories. Common bread contains large quantities of sodium and calcium, and as many as 275 calories per 3 1/2 oz. (100 grams).*

EASY

**4 servings**
Preparation time: **5 minutes**
Cooking time: **10 minutes**
Calories per serving: **190**

**14 oz. (400 g) tomatoes, ripe**
**1 clove of garlic**
**1 onion**
**3 sprigs parsley**
**8 slices white bread**

*1.* Wash and chop the tomatoes, then drain the excess liquid in a strainer for five minutes. Peel and mince the garlic and onion.

*2.* Cook the tomatoes with the garlic and onion in a non-stick pan for about 10 minutes, on low heat. Mix often and allow the liquid to reduce by half.

*3.* Once cooked, purée the tomatoes in a food mill so as to remove the skin and seeds. Transfer the sauce into a bowl.

*4.* Clean, wash and mince the parsley, keeping a sprig aside as garnish.

*5.* Toast the sliced ??bread on the grill or in the oven.

*6.* Serve the sauce, garnished with parsley and warm toast (this can be wrapped it in a napkin to keep it warm). In addition to toast, the sauce can also be used to flavor meat, fish or boiled vegetables.

# WALNUT CREAM SAUCE

*Walnuts are rich in omega-3 fatty acids and help prevent heart and eye diseases. Walnut oil is recommended in patients suffering from maculopathy (a condition of the eye). They also contain large quantities of vitamin B and dietary minerals, as well as plenty of calcium, potassium, phosphorus and zinc. Other vitamins worthy of note are vitamin E, folic acid and retinol. Walnuts also prevent ageing and degenerative diseases, as well as monitoring the level of cholesterol in the blood. But beware: 3 1/2 oz. (100 grams) of walnuts are equivalent to 660 calories.*

EASY

**4 servings**
Preparation time: **5 minutes**
Calories per serving: **195**

*1.* In a mortar, finely crush the walnuts (keeping some aside as garnish) and transfer the mixture into a bowl. With oilseeds, it is always best to use the mortar rather than the blender, so as not to heat the oil they contain and spoil their flavor.

*2.* Pour the cream and the ricotta cheese into the same bowl and mix with a fork until the mixture is smooth. Add salt and pepper to taste.

*3.* Transfer the mixture into a bowl and garnish with the remaining walnuts. This cream sauce is perfect as an appetiser, spread on bread or as a condiment for pasta or rice.

1 3/4 oz. (50 g) walnuts, shelled
1/2 cup (100 g) soy cream
3 1/2 oz. (100 g) sheep milk ricotta
Salt
Pepper

# CHILLI PEPPER AND TOMATO CREAM SAUCE

*Like all other tomatoes, beef tomatoes contain vitamins A and E, as well as lycopenes and beta-carotene, and are excellent antioxidants. All of these substances are well known for their ability to prevent cancer and degenerative diseases. They help the heart and blood circulation, as well as improving eye sight. This variety of tomatoes is particularly tasty raw: it's thin skin is easy to remove, and it rich, tender pulp has very few seeds.*

 EASY

**4 servings**
Preparation time: **10 minutes**
Calories per serving: **20**

4 beef tomatoes
2 sweet chilli peppers
2 spicy chilli peppers, fresh
10 basil leaves
Salt

*1.* Wash, slice, seed and peel the tomatoes, keeping the fillets. Sieve the excess liquid.

*2.* Wash, dry and slice the sweet and spicy chilli peppers: for a particularly spicy sauce, leave the seeds of the latter; otherwise remove them.

*3.* Wash, dry and mince the basil, keeping a few leaves aside as garnish.

*4.* Put the ingredients in the blender, add salt to taste and blend at low speed until well mixed but lumpy.

*5.* Transfer the mixture into a bowl, garnishing with two basil leaves. ? Use the sauce to flavor vegetables, pasta, rice, steaks or fish fillets. The sauce is also excellent spread on bread, as a snack or appetiser. As it contains no oil, it should be consumed quickly, storing it in the refrigerator for at the most one day.

# SESAME CREAM SAUCE

*Sesame seeds are rich in amino acids and vitamins (D, E, A and B-complex) and contain a considerable amount of calcium, as well as minerals such as zinc, phosphorus, selenium, potassium, copper and magnesium: zinc and selenium, in particular, have effective antioxidant properties. Due to their unsaturated fats, such as linoleic acid and omega-3, these seeds are very useful for preventing vascular diseases. They also stimulate immune resistance and can be taken in convalescence to aid recovery from physical illness.*

EASY

**4 servings**
Preparation time: **10 minutes**
Calories per serving: **320**

*1.* Toast the sesame seeds in a non-stick pan for around 2 minutes, shaking often to prevent them from burning or turning bitter.

*2.* Grind them gently and coarsely in a mortar.

*3.* Pour the seeds into a bowl, add the ricotta cheese and stir until the mixture is smooth. Add salt and pepper to taste, and stir.

*4.* Transfer the cream sauce into a gravy boat and serve with toasted bread, croutons or breadsticks. The sauce is ideal as an appetizer or as a rich and flavorsome starter. It can be stored in the refrigerator for several days.

**1 1/4 cup (200 g) light sesame seeds**
**3 1/2 oz. (100 g) fresh ricotta**
**Salt**
**Pepper**

# TURMERIC AND FLAXSEED CREAM SAUCE

*Flax seeds are high in omega-3 fatty acids, dietary minerals, proteins, lipids, linoleic acid and fibres. They boast significant antioxidant properties and also help improve blood circulation. Furthermore, omega-3 also has a healthy effect on the heart, and a spoonful of flax seeds contains as many as 1.7 grams! It is thought that flax seeds may reduce the risk of developing breast, prostate and colon cancer.*

EASY

**4 servings**
Preparation time: **10 minutes**
Calories per serving: **69**

1. In a saucepan, pour two tablespoons of water, then add the turmeric and bring to a boil, stirring constantly so that it does not stick.

2. Let cool and add the soy cream, then stir again.

3. Toast the flax seeds for a few minutes in a non-stick pan, on high heat, shaking often to keep the seeds from burning.

4. Transfer all the ingredients into a bowl, keeping aside half a teaspoon of flax seeds as garnish, and stir well.

5. When serving, transfer the mixture into small bowls and garnish with the flax seeds. This turmeric cream sauce is a great flavor enhancer for stewed vegetables, grilled meats, boiled fish and pulses. It can be stored in the refrigerator for two or three days.

1 tbsp turmeric
1/2 cup (100 g) soy cream
2 tbsp (20 g) flax seeds

# TUNA CREAM SAUCE
# WITH COGNAC AND PUMPKIN SEEDS

*Pumpkin seeds are rich in protein (18.7%) and carbohydrates (24%). They contain various dietary minerals, as well as a considerable quantity of zinc and phosphorus, and substances such as cucurbitin, delta-sterol, phytosterol, plant globulins, and vitamins F and E. The latter perform a significant antioxidant and cell membrane protection action.*

EASY

**4 servings**
Preparation time: **10 minutes**
Resting time: **20 minutes**
Calories per serving: **200**

1. Remove the tuna from the tin and let it drain, then place it in a blender with the cognac and freshly squeezed lemon juice. Season with salt and pepper to taste, and blend until the mixture is smooth. Join half the pumpkin seeds, pour the mixture into a gravy boat and leave to rest in the freezer for 20 minutes.

2. Meanwhile, cut the bread into strips and toast it in the oven for about 10 minutes at 400° F (200° C). Allow to cool at room temperature.

3. When ready to serve, take the cream sauce out of the freezer, garnish it with pumpkin seeds and serve with the toasted bread. The tuna cream sauce is a perfect accompaniment to boiled eggs and steamed courgettes. Spread on bread, it makes for a great snack or a tasty appetiser.

3 1/2 oz. (100 g) tuna in brine
1/4 cup (50 ml) cognac
Juice of 1 lemon
2 tbsp (20 g) pumpkin seeds
7 oz. (200 g) home made bread
Salt
Pepper

# YOGHURT WITH ONIONS, CUCUMBER AND CHILLI PEPPER

*Cucumber is the fruit of the plant by the same name. Native to northern India, it has been used in southern Europe for thousands of years. It contains vitamin A and C, various trace elements and plenty of tartaric acid, which reduces the absorption of sugars into the intestine, and is therefore suitable for low-calorie diets. It has very few calories and considerable diuretic and detoxifying properties.*

EASY

**4 servings**
Preparation time: **5 minutes**
Calories per serving: **46**

1. Peel and thinly slice the onion. Trim and wash the cucumber, then cut it into rounds. Cut the chilli pepper into rounds: remember that it is the seeds that give this fruit its spicy flavor, so decide whether or not to discard them, depending on how hot you want the dish to be.

2. Pour the yoghurt and vegetables into a bowl, keeping a few pieces of each vegetable aside as garnish. Season with salt and pepper to taste, then stir.

3. Transfer the mixture into a gravy boat and garnish with the vegetable pieces at will. This is a light, refreshing and thirst-quenching dressing, perfect in the summer months and in particularly hot weather. Although easy to prepare, the sauce is very tasty, especially served with salads, and vegetables, both fresh or boiled, such as potatoes.

**2 cups (500 ml) low-fat natural yoghurt**
**1 cucumber**
**1 chilli pepper, fresh**
**1 red onion**
**Salt**
**Pepper**

# FAT CONTENT

## FAT CONTENT PER 100 GRAMS OF PRODUCT

Clearly the fat content is not, in itself, a conclusive indicator. What is more important is the balance between fats: saturated, unsaturated or trans fats.

| | | | | |
|---|---|---|---|---|
| Agar seaweed | 0.03 | Breadcrumbs | 5.48 |
| Almond oil | 100 | Bresaola | 1.94 |
| Almont nougat | 1.67 | Brewer's yeast | 1.90 |
| Anchovies | 4.84 | Broccoli | 0.37 |
| Apricots | 0.39 | Buckwheat | 3.40 |
| Artichokes | 0.15 | Butter | 81.11 |
| Asparagus paste | 3.26 | Caciotta sheep`s cheese | 29.84 |
| Asparagus | 0.22 | Cane sugar | 0 |
| Asparagus | 0.42 | Cannellini beans | 1.50 |
| Avocado | 10.06 | Capers | 0.86 |
| Baby biscuits | 4.20 | Capon | 5.40 |
| Bagel | 1.72 | Cardoon (artichoke thistle) | 0.11 |
| Baking powder | 0.80 | Carob flour | 0.65 |
| Baking yeast | 0 | Carp | 5.60 |
| Bamboo | 0.22 | Carrots | 0.24 |
| Bamboo | 0.30 | Catfish | 2.82 |
| Barley flour | 1.84 | Cauliflower | 0.28 |
| Basil | 0.64 | Caviar | 17.90 |
| Beer | 0 | Celery paste | 4.46 |
| Black beans | 1.42 | Celery | 0.19 |
| Black pepper | 3.26 | Celery | 0.30 |
| Blackberry juice | 0.60 | Chard | 0.20 |
| Boiled apple | 0.36 | Chicken livers | 4.83 |
| Boiled artichokes | 0.36 | Chickpeas | 6.04 |
| Boiled aubergine | 0.23 | Chilli con carne | 3.27 |
| Boiled beetroot | 0.18 | Chives | 0.70 |
| Boiled borlotti beans | 0.65 | Chocolate ice-cream | 11.00 |
| Boiled broccoli | 0.41 | Chocolate milkshake | 2.70 |
| Boiled cabbage | 0.09 | Cinnamon cake | 1.70 |
| Boiled cannellini beans | 0.62 | Clams | 0.96 |
| Boiled carrots | 0.18 | Clementines | 0.15 |
| Boiled chestnuts | 1.38 | Common wheat | 1.99 |
| Boiled courgettes | 0.36 | Cocoa butter | 100 |
| Boiled frozen carrots | 0.68 | Coconut oil | 100 |
| Boiled onions | 0.19 | Cold vanilla yoghurt | 5.60 |
| Boiled peppers | 0.20 | Cooked apple | 0.42 |
| Boiled sweets | 8.10 | Cooked barley | 0.44 |
| Borage | 0.81 | Cooked beef ossobuco | 4.33 |
| Bottled piña colada | 7.60 | Cooked beef steak | 7.18 |
| Bread croutons | 1.30 | Cooked bran | 0.86 |
| Bread made from type 0 flour | 3.50 | Cooked burbot` | 1.04 |
| Bread with raisins | 4.40 | Cooked cod | 0.86 |

| | |
|---|---|
| Cooked Courgette flowers | 0.08 |
| Cooked eel | 14.95 |
| Cooked egg pasta | 1.74 |
| Cooked egg tagliolini pasta | 2.07 |
| Cooked grey mullet | 4.86 |
| Cooked grouper | 1.30 |
| Cooked halibut | 1.61 |
| Cooked kamut | 0.91 |
| Cooked lobster | 0.86 |
| Cooked mackerel | 17.81 |
| Cooked millet | 1.00 |
| Cooked mussels | 4.48 |
| Cooked octopus | 7.48 |
| Cooked ostrich meat | 7.07 |
| Cooked oysters | 3.42 |
| Cooked perch | 1.18 |
| Cooked prawns | 1.70 |
| Cooked ray | 0.90 |
| Cooked rice | 0.19 |
| Cooked salmon | 8.23 |
| Cooked sole | 2.37 |
| Cooked spaghetti | 0.93 |
| Cooked swordfish | 7.93 |
| Cooked T-bone steak | 17.12 |
| Cooked tomatoes | 0.11 |
| Cooked trout | 7.38 |
| Cooked veal loin | 4.65 |
| Cooked wholemeal macaroni | 0.54 |
| Cooked wholemeal spaghetti | 0.54 |
| Corn flakes | 0.59 |
| Courgette flowers | 0.40 |
| Courgettes | 0.40 |
| Crackers | 20.60 |
| Cream cake | 8.50 |
| Cream | 35.00 |
| Crème caramel | 4.03 |
| Cress | 0.70 |
| Crisps | 36.40 |
| Crispy chocolate cereal | 2.90 |
| Croissants | 21.00 |
| Dark chocolate | 34.20 |
| Decaffeinated coffee | 0 |

| | |
|---|---|
| Decaffeinated tea | 0 |
| Dill | 1.12 |
| Dried apricots | 0.62 |
| Dried banana | 1.81 |
| Dried basil | 4.07 |
| Dried beef | 1.94 |
| Dried carrots | 1.49 |
| Dried chestnuts | 4.45 |
| Dried chilli peppers | 5.81 |
| Dried dates | 0.39 |
| Dried figs | 0.40 |
| Dried jujubes | 1.11 |
| Dried lychees | 1.20 |
| Dried marjoram | 7.04 |
| Dried mint | 6.03 |
| Dried mushrooms | 0.99 |
| Dried parsley | 5.48 |
| Dried pine nuts | 68.37 |
| Dried prunes | 0.38 |
| Dried spirulina seaweed | 7.72 |
| Dried tomatoes | 2.97 |
| Durum wheat | 1.71 |
| Egg bread | 6.00 |
| Egg yolk | 55.80 |
| Emmenthal cheese | 27.80 |
| Endives | 0.20 |
| Espresso coffee | 0.18 |
| Farmed mushrooms | 0.36 |
| Fava beans | 0.22 |
| Feta cheese | 21.28 |
| Fillet of pork | 2.17 |
| Fish meatballs | 1.73 |
| Fish stock | 0.60 |
| Focaccia bread with onion | 1.60 |
| Focaccia bread with raisins | 4.40 |
| Foccacia bread with sesame | 1.62 |
| Fontina cheese | 31.14 |
| French baguette | 2.14 |
| Fresh amarena cherries | 0.30 |
| Fresh aubergine | 0.19 |
| Fresh borlotti beans | 1.23 |
| Fresh celery | 0.17 |

| | | | |
|---|---|---|---|
| Fresh cherries | 0.20 | Lean Parma ham | 5.71 |
| Fresh cranberries | 0.14 | Lean veal | 2.59 |
| Fresh egg | 0.17 | Leeks | 0.20 |
| Fresh mint | 0.73 | Leeks | 0.30 |
| Fresh peas | 0.20 | Lemon juice | 0.24 |
| Fresh rosemary | 5.86 | Lemon tea with sugar | 0.30 |
| Fresh thyme | 1.68 | Lemons | 0.30 |
| Fresh tomatoes | 0.20 | Lentils | 1.06 |
| Fried and salted potato chips | 5.22 | Lettuce | 0.22 |
| Frog's legs | 0.30 | Lettuce | 0.30 |
| Frozen amarena cherries | 0.43 | Long grain rice | 0.66 |
| Frozen blackberries | 0.43 | Loquats | 0.20 |
| Frozen French bread | 6.10 | Lupini beans | 2.92 |
| Frozen spinach | 0.57 | Macaroni bolognese | 1.47 |
| Fruit ice-cream without sugar | 0.10 | Mackerel conserved in oil | 10.12 |
| Gin | 0 | Mandarins | 0.32 |
| Goat's milk | 4.14 | Mango | 0.38 |
| Gorgonzola cheese | 28.74 | Manioca | 0.28 |
| Grape juice | 0 | Margarine | 80.71 |
| Grapefruit juice | 0.13 | Marshmallow | 0.20 |
| Grapefruit | 0.14 | Mascarpone cheese | 47.00 |
| Green and red peppers | 0.30 | Mashed potato | 4.22 |
| Green beans | 0.22 | Mayonnaise | 77.80 |
| Green radicchio | 0.22 | Meat-filled ravioli bolognese | 74 |
| Grilled beef steak | 7.68 | Melon | 0.19 |
| Groats and meal | 1.05 | Milk chocolate with almonds | 34.40 |
| Ground ginger | 4.24 | Millet | 4.22 |
| Gruyere cheese | 32.34 | Miso soup | 6.01 |
| Hamburger | 11.24 | Moka coffee | 0.03 |
| Hazelnuts | 62.40 | Mozzarella cheese | 22.35 |
| Hen | 2.47 | Muesli | 5.50 |
| Home made egg-free pasta | 0.98 | Muffins | 11.40 |
| Home-made zucotto dessert | 4.30 | Mulberries | 0.39 |
| Honey tarts | 11.00 | Multi-seed oil | 100 |
| Honey | 0 | Mushroom paste | 5.89 |
| Horse meat | 6.05 | Mushroom sauce | 2.71 |
| Hot chilli pepper | 0.44 | Nectarines | 0.32 |
| Ice cream cones with sugar | 3.80 | New potatoes | 0.10 |
| Instant cappucino sweetened | 5.56 | Nutella | 32.40 |
| Instant tea without sugar | 0.18 | Oat bread | 4.40 |
| Jam biscuits | 16.30 | Octopus | 1.38 |
| Lard | 100 | Olive oil | 100 |

| | | | |
|---|---|---|---|
| Onion paste | 4.20 | Pre-cooked tinned beans | 0.37 |
| Onion sauce | 3.00 | Raisins | 0.20 |
| Orange (or lemon) sorbet | 2.00 | Rapini leaves | 0.42 |
| Orange and mandarin juice | 0.20 | Raspberries | 0.65 |
| Orange juice | 0 | Raspberry | 0.28 |
| Orange carrot and lemon juice | 0.01 | Raw banana | 0.37 |
| Oranges | 0.30 | Raw beef | 30.00 |
| Oregano | 4.28 | Raw fava beans | 0.70 |
| Organic apricot jam | 0.20 | Raw horse meat | 4.60 |
| Organic fruit jam | 0.07 | Raw spaghetti | 1.51 |
| Organic lemons | 0 | Raw veal | 2.50 |
| Organic tomato juice | 0.05 | Raw wholemeal macaroni | 1.40 |
| Ovaltine | 1.33 | Red mullet | 3.79 |
| Oven-baked potatoes | 0.10 | Red radicchio | 0.25 |
| Ovuli mushrooms | 0.29 | Red salmon | 4.40 |
| Palm oil | 100 | Rhubarb | 0.20 |
| Pancetta | 45.04 | Rice flour | 1.42 |
| Papaya | 0.26 | Roast chicken breast | 3.54 |
| Parboiled rice | 0.37 | Roast chicken | 20.97 |
| Parma ham | 18.52 | Roast potatoes | 0.15 |
| Passion fruit | 0.70 | Roasted chestnuts | 2.20 |
| Peaches | 0.25 | Roasted veal loin | 3.39 |
| Peanut oil | 100 | Roasted venison | 3.19 |
| Peanuts | 49.24 | Rocket | 0.66 |
| Pears | 0.12 | Roquefort cheese | 30.64 |
| Peas | 0.30 | Rye bread | 3.30 |
| Peas | 0.40 | Rye flour | 1.52 |
| Pecorino cheese | 26.94 | Saffron | 5.85 |
| Persimmon | 0.19 | Sake | 0 |
| Pheasant (thigh) | 4.30 | Salami | 31.10 |
| Pickled gherkins | 0.19 | Salmon | 10.43 |
| Pike | 1.22 | Salt | 0 |
| Pineapple and pineapple juice | 0.12 | Salted cod | 2.37 |
| Pistachio nuts | 45.39 | Salted jellyfish | 1.40 |
| Pomegranate | 1.17 | Sardines | 4.50 |
| Popcorn | 4.54 | Scallops | 0.84 |
| Porcini mushrooms | 0.10 | Scrambled egg | 10.98 |
| Pork mortadella | 35.80 | Sea bass | 2.56 |
| Pork sausage | 53.10 | Sea pike | 0.69 |
| Potato salad | 8.20 | Sea snails | 1.40 |
| Potato soup | 3. 10 | Semi-skimmed natural yoghurt | 0.18 |
| Powdered garlic | 0.73 | Shrimps | 1.47 |

| | | | | |
|---|---|---|---|---|
| Sieved tomato | 0.21 | Tortillas | 2.85 |
| Skimmed milk | 0.08 | Tuna in brine | 0.82 |
| Smoked ham | 9.02 | Turkey | 4.79 |
| Smoked salmon | 4.32 | Turkey breast | 8.30 |
| Smoked sturgeon | 4.40 | Turmeric | 9.88 |
| Soy milk | 1.99 | Turnip and radish | 0.24 |
| Soybean oil | 100 | UHT whole milk | 3.66 |
| Spinach | 0.26 | Uncooked cous cous | 0.64 |
| Spinach | 0.39 | Uncooked kamut | 2.20 |
| Spirulina seaweed | 0.39 | Unsweetened cocoa | 13.67 |
| Stewed crab | 1.54 | Vanilla extract | 0.06 |
| Stewed cuttlefish | 1.40 | Vanilla milkshake | 3.03 |
| Stewed lobster | 1.94 | Vanilla or banana pudding | 0.60 |
| Stewed octopus | 2.08 | Vinegar | 0 |
| Stewed prawns | 1.30 | Wakame (seaweed) | 0.64 |
| Stewed rabbit | 8.41 | Walnut oil | 100 |
| Strawberries | 0.30 | Walnuts | 65.21 |
| Strawberry ice-cream | 8.40 | Wasabi | 0.63 |
| Sturgeon | 4.04 | Water | 0 |
| Sugared almonds | 17.93 | Watermelon | 0.15 |
| Sugar-free chewing gum | 0.40 | Wheat bran | 4.25 |
| Sunflower oil | 100 | Wheat Bread | 3.90 |
| Surimi | 0.90 | Whisky | 0 |
| Sweet gerkins | 0.41 | White low-fat bread | 2.50 |
| Sweet onions | 0.08 | White pepper | 2.12 |
| Sweet or salted white corn | 1.41 | Whole bran bread | 4.40 |
| Sweetened cranberries | 1.37 | Whole milk yoghurt | 3.25 |
| Tacos | 20.83 | Whole milk | 3.25 |
| Tamarind | 0.60 | Wholegrain rice | 2.92 |
| Tapioca | 0.02 | Wild apples | 0.30 |
| Tinned cherries | 0.21 | Wild asparagus | 0.20 |
| Tinned chilli and beans | 5.26 | Wild blueberries | 0.76 |
| Tinned pasta bolognese | 5.10 | Wild figs | 0.30 |
| Tinned peeled tomatoes | 0.13 | Wild prunes | 0.28 |
| Tinned pumpkin | 0.28 | Wine | 0 |
| Toasted oatmeal bread | 4.80 | Yellow or white corn | 4.74 |
| Tofu yoghurt | 1.80 | Yellow peppers | 0.21 |
| Tofu | 20.18 | Yellow pumpkin | 0.10 |
| Tofu | 8.72 | Yellow radishes | 0.20 |
| Tonic water | 0 | Yellow tomatoes | 0.26 |

# IN DECREASING ORDER

## FAT CONTENT PER 100 GRAMS OF PRODUCT

Clearly the fat content is not, in itself, a conclusive indicator. What is more important is the balance between fats: saturated, unsaturated or trans fats.

| | | | |
|---|---|---|---|
| Almond oil | 100 | Tacos | 20.83 |
| Cocoa butter | 100 | Crackers | 20.60 |
| Coconut oil | 100 | Tofu | 20.18 |
| Lard | 100 | Parma ham | 18.52 |
| Multi-seed oil | 100 | Sugared almonds | 17.93 |
| Olive oil | 100 | Caviar | 17.90 |
| Palm oil | 100 | Cooked mackerel | 17.81 |
| Peanut oil | 100 | Cooked T-bone steak | 17.12 |
| Soybean oil | 100 | Jam biscuits | 16.30 |
| Sunflower oil | 100 | Cooked eel | 14.95 |
| Walnut oil | 100 | Unsweetened cocoa | 13.67 |
| Butter | 81.11 | Muffins | 11.40 |
| Margarine | 80.71 | Hamburger | 11.24 |
| Mayonnaise | 77.80 | Chocolate ice-cream | 11.00 |
| Dried pine nuts | 68.37 | Honey tarts | 11.00 |
| Walnuts | 65.21 | Scrambled egg | 10.98 |
| Hazelnuts | 62.40 | Salmon | 10.43 |
| Egg yolk | 55.80 | Mackerel conserved in oil | 10.12 |
| Pork sausage | 53.10 | Avocado | 10.06 |
| Peanuts | 49.24 | Turmeric | 9.88 |
| Mascarpone cheese | 47.00 | Smoked ham | 9.02 |
| Pistachio nuts | 45.39 | Tofu | 8.72 |
| Pancetta | 45.04 | Cream cake | 8.50 |
| Crisps | 36.40 | Stewed rabbit | 8.41 |
| Pork mortadella | 35.80 | Strawberry ice-cream | 8.40 |
| Cream | 35.00 | Turkey breast | 8.30 |
| Milk chocolate with almonds | 34.40 | Cooked salmon | 8.23 |
| Dark chocolate | 34.20 | Potato salad | 8.20 |
| Nutella | 32.40 | Boiled sweets | 8.10 |
| Gruyère cheese | 32.34 | Cooked swordfish | 7.93 |
| Fontina cheese | 31.14 | Dried spirulina seaweed | 7.72 |
| Salami | 31.10 | Grilled beef steak | 7.68 |
| Roquefort cheese | 30.64 | Bottled pina colada | 7.60 |
| Raw beef | 30.00 | Cooked octopus | 7.48 |
| Caciotta sheep's cheese | 29.84 | Cooked trout | 7.38 |
| Gorgonzola cheese | 28.74 | Cooked beef steak | 7.18 |
| Emmenthal cheese | 27.80 | Cooked ostrich meat | 7.07 |
| Pecorino cheese | 26.94 | Dried marjoram | 7.04 |
| Mozzarella cheese | 22.35 | Frozen French bread | 6.10 |
| Feta cheese | 21.28 | Horse meat | 6.05 |
| Croissants | 21.00 | Chickpeas | 6.04 |
| Roast chicken | 20.97 | Dried mint | 6.03 |

| | | | |
|---|---|---|---|
| Miso soup | 6.01 | Ground ginger | 4.24 |
| Egg bread | 6.00 | Mashed potato | 4.22 |
| Mushroom paste | 5.89 | Millet | 4.22 |
| Fresh rosemary | 5.86 | Baby biscuits | 4.20 |
| Saffron | 5.85 | Onion paste | 4.20 |
| Dried chilli peppers | 5.81 | Goat's milk | 4.14 |
| Lean Parma ham | 5.71 | Dried basil | 4.07 |
| Carp | 5.60 | Sturgeon | 4.04 |
| Cold vanilla yoghurt | 5.60 | Crème caramel | 4.03 |
| Instant cappucino sweetened | 5.56 | Wheat Bread | 3.90 |
| Muesli | 5.50 | Ice cream cones with sugar | 3.80 |
| Breadcrumbs | 5.48 | Red mullet | 3.79 |
| Dried parsley | 5.48 | UHT whole milk | 3.66 |
| Capon | 5.40 | Roast chicken breast | 3.54 |
| Tinned chilli and beans | 5.26 | Bread made from type 0 flour | 3.50 |
| Fried and salted potato chips | 5.22 | Cooked oysters | 3.42 |
| Tinned pasta bolognese | 5.10 | Buckwheat | 3.40 |
| Cooked grey mullet | 4.86 | Roasted veal loin | 3.39 |
| Anchovies | 4.84 | Rye bread | 3.30 |
| Chicken livers | 4.83 | Chilli con carne | 3.27 |
| Toasted oatmeal bread | 4.80 | Asparagus paste | 3.26 |
| Turkey | 4.79 | Black pepper | 3.26 |
| Yellow or white corn | 4.74 | Whole milk yoghurt | 3.25 |
| Cooked veal loin | 4.65 | Whole milk | 3.25 |
| Raw horse meat | 4.60 | Roasted venison | 3.19 |
| Popcorn | 4.54 | Potato soup | 3.10 |
| Sardines | 4.50 | Vanilla milkshake | 3.03 |
| Cooked mussels | 4.48 | Onion sauce | 3.00 |
| Celery paste | 4.46 | Dried tomatoes | 2.97 |
| Dried chestnuts | 4.45 | Lupini beans | 2.92 |
| Bread with raisins | 4.40 | Wholegrain rice | 2.92 |
| Focaccia bread with raisins | 4.40 | Crispy chocolate cereal | 2.90 |
| Oat bread | 4.40 | Tortillas | 2.85 |
| Red salmon | 4.40 | Catfish | 2.82 |
| Smoked sturgeon | 4.40 | Mushroom sauce | 2.71 |
| Whole bran bread | 4.40 | Chocolate milkshake | 2.70 |
| Cooked beef ossobuco | 4.33 | Lean veal | 2.59 |
| Smoked salmon | 4.32 | Sea bass | 2.56 |
| Home-made zucotto dessert | 4.30 | Raw veal | 2.50 |
| Pheasant (thigh) | 4.30 | White low-fat bread | 2.50 |
| Oregano | 4.28 | Hen | 2.47 |
| Wheat bran | 4.25 | Cooked sole | 2.37 |

| | | | | |
|---|---|---|---|
| Salted cod | 2.37 | Salted jellyfish | 1.40 |
| Sea bass | 2.33 | Sea snails | 1.40 |
| Roasted chestnuts | 2.20 | Stewed cuttlefish | 1.40 |
| Uncooked kamut | 2.20 | Boiled chestnuts | 1.38 |
| Fillet of pork | 2.17 | Octopus | 1.38 |
| French baguette | 2.14 | Sweetened cranberries | 1.37 |
| White pepper | 2.12 | Ovaltine | 1.33 |
| Stewed octopus | 2.08 | Bread croutons | 1.30 |
| Cooked egg Tagliolini pasta | 2.07 | Cooked grouper | 1.30 |
| Orange (or lemon) sorbet | 2.00 | Stewed prawns | 1.30 |
| Common wheat | 1.99 | Fresh borlotti beans | 1.23 |
| Soy milk | 1.99 | Pike | 1.22 |
| Bresaola | 1.94 | Dried lychees | 1.20 |
| Dried beef | 1.94 | Cooked perch | 1.18 |
| Stewed lobster | 1.94 | Pomegranate | 1.17 |
| Brewer's yeast | 1.90 | Dill | 1.12 |
| Barley flour | 1.84 | Dried jujubes | 1.11 |
| Dried banana | 1.81 | Lentils | 1.06 |
| Tofu yoghurt | 1.80 | Groats and meal | 1.05 |
| Cooked egg pasta | 1.74 | Cooked burbot | 1.04 |
| Meat-filled ravioli bolognese | 1.74 | Cooked millet | 1.00 |
| Fish meatballs | 1.73 | Dried mushrooms | 0.99 |
| Bagel | 1.72 | Home made egg-free pasta | 0.98 |
| Durum wheat | 1.71 | Clams | 0.96 |
| Cinnamon cake | 1.70 | Cooked spaghetti | 0.93 |
| Cooked prawns | 1.70 | Cooked kamut | 0.91 |
| Fresh thyme | 1.68 | Cooked ray | 0.90 |
| Almont nougat | 1.67 | Surimi | 0.90 |
| Foccacia bread with sesame | 1.62 | Capers | 0.86 |
| Cooked halibut | 1.61 | Cooked bran | 0.86 |
| Focaccia bread with onion | 1.60 | Cooked cod | 0.86 |
| Stewed crab | 1.54 | Cooked lobster | 0.86 |
| Rye flour | 1.52 | Scallops | 0.84 |
| Raw spaghetti | 1.51 | Tuna in brine | 0.82 |
| Cannellini beans | 1.50 | Borage | 0.81 |
| Dried carrots | 1.49 | Baking powder | 0.80 |
| Macaroni bolognese | 1.47 | Wild blueberries | 0.76 |
| Shrimps | 1.47 | Fresh mint | 0.73 |
| Black beans | 1.42 | Powdered garlic | 0.73 |
| Rice flour | 1.42 | Chives | 0.70 |
| Sweet or salted white corn | 1.41 | Cress | 0.70 |
| Raw wholemeal macaroni | 1.40 | Passion fruit | 0.70 |

| | | | |
|---|---|---|---|
| Raw fava beans | 0.70 | Mango | 0.38 |
| Sea pike | 0.69 | Broccoli | 0.37 |
| Boiled frozen carrots | 0.68 | Parboiled rice | 0.37 |
| Long grain rice | 0.66 | Pre-cooked tinned beans | 0.37 |
| Rocket | 0.66 | Raw banana | 0.37 |
| Boiled borlotti beans | 0.65 | Boiled apple | 0.36 |
| Carob flour | 0.65 | Boiled artichokes | 0.36 |
| Raspberries | 0.65 | Boiled courgettes | 0.36 |
| Basil | 0.64 | Farmed mushrooms | 0.36 |
| Uncooked cous cous | 0.64 | Mandarins | 0.32 |
| Wakame (seaweed) | 0.64 | Nectarines | 0.32 |
| Wasabi | 0.63 | Bamboo | 0.30 |
| Boiled cannellini beans | 0.62 | Wild apples | 0.30 |
| Dried apricots | 0.62 | Celery | 0.30 |
| Blackberry juice | 0.60 | Fresh amarena cherries | 0.30 |
| Fish stock | 0.60 | Frog's legs | 0.30 |
| Tamarind | 0.60 | Green and red peppers | 0.30 |
| Vanilla or banana pudding | 0.60 | Leeks | 0.30 |
| Corn flakes | 0.59 | Lemon tea with sugar | 0.30 |
| Frozen spinach | 0.57 | Lemons | 0.30 |
| Cooked wholemeal macaroni | 0.54 | Lettuce | 0.30 |
| Cooked wholemeal spaghetti | 0.54 | Oranges | 0.30 |
| Cooked barley | 0.44 | Peas | 0.30 |
| Hot chilli pepper | 0.44 | Strawberries | 0.30 |
| Frozen amarena cherries | 0.43 | Wild figs | 0.30 |
| Frozen blackberries | 0.43 | Ovuli mushrooms | 0.29 |
| Asparagus | 0.42 | Cauliflower | 0.28 |
| Cooked apple | 0.42 | Manioca | 0.28 |
| | | Raspberry | 0.28 |
| Boiled broccoli | 0.41 | Tinned pumpkin | 0.28 |
| Sweet gerkins | 0.41 | Wild prunes | 0.28 |
| Courgette flowers | 0.40 | Papaya | 0.26 |
| Courgettes | 0.40 | Spinach | 0.26 |
| Dried figs | 0.40 | Yellow tomatoes | 0.26 |
| Peas | 0.40 | Peaches | 0.25 |
| Sugar-free chewing gum | 0.40 | Red radicchio | 0.25 |
| Apricots | 0.39 | Carrots | 0.24 |
| Dried dates | 0.39 | Lemon juice | 0.24 |
| Mulberries | 0.39 | Turnip and radish | 0.24 |
| Spinach | 0.39 | Boiled aubergine | 0.23 |
| Spirulina seaweed | 0.39 | Asparagus | 0.22 |
| Dried prunes | 0.38 | Bamboo | 0.22 |

| | | | | |
|---|---|---|---|---|
| Fava beans | 0.22 | Grapefruit juice | 0.13 |
| Green beans | 0.22 | Tinned peeled tomatoes | 0.13 |
| Green radicchio | 0.22 | Oranges | 0.12 |
| Lettuce | 0.22 | Pears | 0.12 |
| Sieved tomato | 0.21 | Pineapple and pineapple juice | 0.12 |
| Tinned cherries | 0.21 | Cardoon (artichoke thistle) | 0.11 |
| Yellow peppers | 0.21 | Cooked tomatoes | 0.11 |
| Boiled peppers | 0.20 | Fruit ice-cream without sugar | 0.10 |
| Chard | 0.20 | New potatoes | 0.10 |
| Endives | 0.20 | Oven-baked potatoes | 0.10 |
| Fresh cherries | 0.20 | Porcini mushrooms | 0.10 |
| Fresh peas | 0.20 | Yellow pumpkin | 0.10 |
| Fresh tomatoes | 0.20 | Boiled cabbage | 0.09 |
| Leeks | 0.20 | Cooked Courgette flowers | 0.08 |
| Loquats | 0.20 | Skimmed milk | 0.08 |
| Marshmallow | 0.20 | Sweet onions | 0.08 |
| Orange and mandarin juice | 0.20 | Organic fruit jam | 0.07 |
| Organic apricot jam | 0.20 | Vanilla extract | 0.06 |
| Raisins | 0.20 | Organic tomato juice | 0.05 |
| Rhubarb | 0.20 | Agar seaweed | 0.03 |
| Wild asparagus | 0.20 | Moka coffee | 0.03 |
| Yellow radishes | 0.20 | Tapioca | 0.02 |
| Boiled onions | 0.19 | Orange carrot and lemon juice | 0.01 |
| Celery | 0.19 | Baking yeast | 0 |
| Cooked rice | 0.19 | Beer | 0 |
| Fresh aubergine | 0.19 | Cane sugar | 0 |
| Melon | 0.19 | Decaffeinated coffee | 0 |
| Persimmon | 0.19 | Decaffeinated tea | 0 |
| Pickled gherkins | 0.19 | Gin | 0 |
| Boiled beetroot | 0.18 | Grape juice | 0 |
| Boiled carrots | 0.18 | Honey | 0 |
| Espresso coffee | 0.18 | Orange juice | 0 |
| Instant tea without sugar | 0.18 | Organic lemons | 0 |
| Semi-skimmed natural yoghurt | 0.18 | Sake | 0 |
| Fresh celery | 0.17 | Salt | 0 |
| Fresh egg | 0.17 | Tonic water | 0 |
| Artichokes | 0.15 | Vinegar | 0 |
| Clementines | 0.15 | Water | 0 |
| Roast potatoes | 0.15 | Whisky | 0 |
| Watermelon | 0.15 | Wine | 0 |
| Fresh cranberries | 0.14 | | |
| Grapefruit | 0.14 | | |

# INDEX

# BIOGRAPHIES OF THE AUTHORS

**Maurizio Cusani** was born in Como and is an ophthalmologist in Milan. Maurizio is interested in the relationship between art, psychology, food and health. To pursue this interest he immersed himself in Sufism and ancient traditions to which he is always attentive, also as an inquisitive traveller. He teaches enneagrams and the symbolism of the human body in naturopathy courses and to Master's degree students of psychosomatics for doctors and psychologists at the Riza institute. He has been deeply interested in food and its repercussions on health for several years. He has written numerous articles on this subject and on nutraceutics, symbolism, Sufism, ancient traditions, psychosomatics and health in general, for various publishers including Riza, Red, Nuova Ipsa and Sagep-La Lontra.

**Cinzia Trenchi** is a naturopath, journalist and freelance photographer specialising in food and enogastronomic itineraries. She brings new recipes and fresh interpretations of cookery books published by Italian and foreign editors. Cinzia is an enthusiastic cook and has been working for many years with various Italian magazines on reviewing regional specialities, traditions, macrobiotics and natural cooking. She provides both the written word and the photos needed to illustrate her creations. An inquisitive traveller, she always tries out local traditional dishes and re-interprets them to match her own sense of taste. Cinzia writes cookery books providing original and creative dishes. She links tastes and tries unusual flavor pairings to experiment with new tastes and to find new ways of pleasing the palate. She never loses sight however of the nutritional aspects of food, and always aims to achieve a good balance between what is served at the table and what is good for the health. She lives in Monferrato, in Piedmont, in a house surrounded by greenery. She uses flowers, aromatic herbs and vegetables from her garden to prepare sauces and original seasonings, not to mention decorations for her dishes. She only uses produce that is in season and is deftly guided by her knowledge of what nature provides.

WHITE STAR PUBLISHERS

WS White Star Publishers® is a registered trademark
property of De Agostini Libri S.p.A.

© 2013 De Agostini Libri S.p.A.
Via G. da Verrazano, 15 - 28100 Novara, Italy
www.whitestar.it - www.deagostini.it

Translation, editing and layout: Soget Srl

ISBN 978-88-544-0756-5
1 2 3 4 5 6   17 16 15 14 13

Printed in China